Mentoring the Educational Leader

A Practical Framework for Success

Kimberly T. Strike
John Nickelsen

ROWMAN & LITTLEFIELD EDUCATION

A division of
ROWMAN & LITTLEFIELD PUBLISHERS, INC.
Lanham • New York • Toronto • Plymouth, UK

Published by Rowman & Littlefield Education
A division of Rowman & Littlefield Publishers, Inc.
A wholly owned subsidiary of The Rowman & Littlefield Publishing Group, Inc.
4501 Forbes Boulevard, Suite 200, Lanham, Maryland 20706
http://www.rowmaneducation.com

Estover Road, Plymouth PL6 7PY, United Kingdom

Copyright © 2011 by Kimberly T. Strike and John Nickelsen

All rights reserved. No part of this book may be reproduced in any form or by any electronic or mechanical means, including information storage and retrieval systems, without written permission from the publisher, except by a reviewer who may quote passages in a review.

British Library Cataloguing in Publication Information Available

Library of Congress Cataloging-in-Publication Data
Strike, Kimberly T., 1966–
  Mentoring the educational leader : a practical framework for success / Kimberly T. Strike, John Nickelsen.
      p. cm.
  Includes bibliographical references.
  ISBN 978-1-61048-286-8 (pbk. : alk. paper) — ISBN 978-1-61048-287-5 (ebook)
  1. Mentoring in education. 2. Educational leadership. 3. School management and organization. 4. School improvement programs. 5. Academic achievement. I. Nickelsen, John R. II. Title.
  LB1731.4.S78 2011
  371.20071'55—dc22   2010044985

♾™ The paper used in this publication meets the minimum requirements of American National Standard for Information Sciences—Permanence of Paper for Printed Library Materials, ANSI/NISO Z39.48-1992.

Printed in the United States of America

To my husband and soul mate, Jeff; to my children: James, Jared, and Elizabeth; and to Edward and Joan Kuper and Jim and Donna Strike. My sincere gratitude for your unconditional love, patience, and support. To Ruth Alles, Emma VanSwol, and John Strike for modeling how to live, love, and laugh.

—Kimberly

To my family: Judy, Andy, Michelle, Drew, Jaden, Matt, Matthew, Myles, Gianna, Lukie, Brookie.

—John

Contents

Foreword vii

Preface ix

Acknowledgments xi

1 The Hierarchy of Mentorship 1

2 Professional Goal Setting 7

3 Leadership Evaluation Tool 13

4 Professional Standards, Personal Life 19

5 Defining Leadership 24

6 Mentoring the Leader 31

7 Understanding School Culture 37

8 Planning 44

9 Starting the School Year: Between the Last Day and Staff Preparation Days 51

10 School Safety and Crisis Management 61

11 Time Management 70

12	Decision Making	77
13	Professional Development and Training	82
14	Testing and Assessment	86
15	Student Achievement	91
16	Behavior Management	98
17	Dealing with the Difficult	104
18	Communication	109
19	Walk-Throughs	114
20	Staff Observations and Evaluations	118
21	Unions and Contracts	123
22	Recognizing Accomplishments	131
23	Programs and Assemblies	138
24	Top Ten List: "What Do You Expect from Your Supervisor?"	143
25	Resources and Support for the Educational Leader	144

| Bibliography | 145 |
| About the Authors | 147 |

Foreword

There is a dearth of pragmatic resources available for the purpose of mentoring educational leaders. At the same time, practitioners have been calling for a "hands-on" guide that can provide focus to aspiring administrators as they thoughtfully and purposefully prepare for their roles as future school leaders. *Mentoring the Educational Leader: A Practical Framework for Success* meets this call. It provides the perfect blend of substance with reflection and activity.

With its conversational writing style, Strike and Nickelsen have made this reader-friendly practitioner guide very useful. They have done a tremendous job of marrying administrative standards from different states and norms of excellence with pragmatic approaches to both leadership and management.

This book is broad in scope, yet quickly delves into the topics at hand. Future administrators and their mentors will be able to move from topic to topic in a way that meets their needs. Sample topics range from start of the school year to decision making, and from working with unions to professional development and evaluation, and from school culture to behavior management.

The format is not prescriptive in nature, but rather allows the mentor and mentee to approach the content in a way suited to meet their individual needs. Perhaps most importantly, they will be able to approach the substance, reflection, and activities in their own school settings and not in a sterile simulated setting.

I think the reader will join me in appreciation of this unique format that uses reflection and activity to command the operational substance of school administrators.

Perry R. Rettig, Ph.D.
Associate Vice Chancellor for Academic Affairs
University of Wisconsin, Oshkosh

Preface

When writing my last book, *Performance and Accountability in Today's Classroom: A Framework for Effective Mentoring*, one of my peer reviewers with many years of experience as a superintendent encouraged me to use the same effective format and write a version for those in educational leadership. The concern was that there wasn't useful material for mentoring the educational leader. In talking with others in the field, this concern was confirmed.

Understanding the importance of collaboration, I teamed up with John Nickelsen, a veteran in the field who has advanced through the ranks in a large urban district. As you read the chapters, you will most likely find a difference in writing styles.

We feel that this complements our goal of recognizing and responding to differences in administrative styles. Some readers will find the technical writing easier to comprehend while others will enjoy the content through writing that resembles a novel. Both styles share knowledge and experience, just differently.

This text is meant to be used as a practical, thorough approach to mentoring the educational leader. The chapters are short. John and I have been in the field long enough to know people (1) don't really care about the theory—they want what they can practice and (2) are short on time.

The format is a few pages of content followed by an activity and then a reflection. The activity and reflection are meant to be a foundation for discussions with one's mentor. Chapters can be read in any order. Think of it as a workbook.

The evaluation tool was created as a culmination of skills good educational leaders should exhibit. The Administrative Standards (or equivalent) of several states were researched and studied. Common threads were extracted, gaps filled in, and descriptive words aligned to create the list within this text.

John and I are very proud of this accomplishment, and thank all those who supported us.

Acknowledgments

Our deepest appreciation goes to our colleagues who acted as eyes and voice throughout the production of this book. With many different backgrounds coming together with a collective focus on providing a quality instruction through effective leadership, we are very proud of the completed project. Thank you to:

Dr. Raymond J. Kuper—Superintendent, Retired, Union Ridge School District 86, Harwood Heights, Illinois
Tom McDonald—Senior Director of Magnet Schools and Fine Arts, Retired, Polk County Schools, Florida
Julie Muellenbach—pre-K4–8 Principal, St. Patrick Parish School, Elkhorn, Wisconsin
Robert Loss—Campus Dean, Northeast Wisconsin Technical College
Doris Loss—Teacher, Retired, Racine Unified School District, Racine, Wisconsin
Students, Parents, Teachers, and Administrators of Racine Unified School District 1964–2002
- Mitchell Middle School
- McKinley Middle School
- Washington Park High School

Racine Unified School District's Central Administration
Larry Gregg—English Teacher, Racine Unified School District
Cathy Pomeranski—Director of Instruction, Elkhorn, Wisconsin, Public School District
Greg Wescott—Superintendent, Elkhorn, Wisconsin, Public School District
Kevin Kitslaar—Assistant Principal, Elkhorn, Wisconsin, Public School District
Cheri Kulland—Principal, Racine Unified School District
Rosalie Daca—Assistant Principal, Racine Unified School District

1

The Hierarchy of Mentorship

Picture yourself—an educator—for a moment, in one of the following situations:

- You have assumed a position totally different from your previous job. Example: Moving from teaching position to administrative position.
- You have moved, keeping your same job, to a new location. Example: Moving from middle school assistant principal to high school assistant principal.
- You have moved from one school district to another.
- You have been promoted. Example: moving from middle school directing principal to district area supervisor.
- You have recently hired a new subordinate. Example: Directing principal hiring an assistant principal.

Who is the mentor?

In each of the above situations, your new immediate supervisor has the obligation to teach you your new job. You need to know a lot in order to meet all your new responsibilities effectively. What, actually, are your responsibilities? What knowledge base do you need? What activities must you perform? With whom must you interact? What deadlines must you meet?

The answers to the above five general questions beg the need for effective mentorship. While roles may change throughout the years—teacher, assistant principal, sub-school principal, directing principal, or district office positions such as curriculum director, district administrator, or superintendent—there are five levels of mentorship. At the beginning of the journey of educational leadership and mentorship, introducing these five levels is appropriate.

First, explore the beginning level. Your supervisor has hired you. Your resume and your interview show that you have the potential of success in your new job.

Your supervisor expects that you can, and will, hit the deck running as soon as you report for duty. So you experience the first form of mentorship. Which is: "I'll tell you what you did wrong after you do it."

In effect, the first level of mentorship, unfortunately, is "Non-Mentorship." Another name might well be "You Made a Mistake."

In this non-mentoring situation, you as a new employee receive no mentoring, either before assuming a new position or during your first few months in the position. As a new assistant principal, for example, having just been promoted, you report for duty two weeks before the start of the school year. Your supervisor, the directing principal, busy with final preparations prior to the first bell on the first day, does not have "time" for formal mentoring.

Your supervisor gives you the list of your initial responsibilities—assigning lockers, putting the finishing touches on the master schedule, completing all remaining transportation issues, writing new lunch room rules, preparing your remarks for the first faculty meeting—just as examples. At the end of the meeting, he says, "Now, if you have any questions, please don't hesitate to ask me."

What happens? You forge ahead on the basis of your acquired knowledge and previous experience. You seek your own mentorship. You ask questions of your peers around the district and of your supervisor. But you still feel that you have been left on your own.

You know from what he said that your supervisor expects you to enter your new position with all knowledge and skills in place. You attempt to think through situations and tasks. You give it your best shot.

Then, after the dust of the first day of school settles, your mentor sits down with you; you turn back the clock, and you begin the mentoring process. But the focus is on "This is what you should have done." After passing that by, you request, and hopefully begin, proactive mentoring.

What results from this level of mentoring? A lot of mistakes, a lot of criticism, and perhaps a lot of trouble. For example, the lunch periods are chaotic. For example, you blow your first student-services hearing.

In sum, you have experienced a negative mentoring experience. You do not learn until you do something wrong or until you figure out what questions you need to ask and then ask them. And, because of no prior mentoring, you have the distinct feeling that you do things wrong all the time.

The examples above present the worst-case scenario: that of no mentoring and that of negative mentoring. The end result is usually chaos. And how does chaos improve teaching and learning? Obviously, it does not. Learning from mistakes is frustrating, to say the very least.

Move now to effective, up-front mentorship.

The second level of mentorship is "Read This." Effective performance in a new job often begins with reading. In some cases, reading is all you need. In most cases, however, reading leads to questions you need answered and into new levels of mentorship.

Here is a good example of using "Read This" mentorship. In midsummer, a new assistant principal reports for work at the middle school. The other assistant principal has several years of experience in the role. (The school has a directing principal and two assistant principals.) As the school's scheduler, the experienced assistant is extremely busy.

The new assistant is brand new: new to the position, new to the district, and new to the school. The new assistant reports for duty at the end of a workday. This is OK. He has just gotten into town and has secured housing for himself and his family. The district has not given him an official start day and time. The school's directing principal has gone home for the day.

Neither the directing principal nor the assistant actually knew when "the new kid" would report. The experienced assistant greets him and tells him that active in-service begins the following day. However, to get him started, the experienced assistant gives him some homework: the list of his duties as the directing principal had designed them, the volume which presents a digest of school district policies, the staff handbook for the school, and last year's student yearbook.

And, like a good college professor, the experienced assistant says, "Read this over tonight. We can cover any questions tomorrow."

The new kid takes the materials home. And the experienced assistant makes a list of all the things the new assistant needs to know in order to prepare for assuming his new responsibility.

Other examples of "Read This" are the student code of responsibilities and rights, the master contract for the school district, copies of suspension letters, copies of completed teacher evaluation forms, and the like. Actually all of these represent introductory readings. Each needs higher levels of mentorship.

Which leads to the third level of mentorship: "I'll Tell You How to . . ." Another name for this level is "Listen to Me." The name is self-explanatory. In this mentorship level, the supervisor tells the new employee how to do something. The employee earnestly takes good notes and asks many questions.

Return to the above example.

Though busy, the experienced assistant and the directing principal make mentoring the new assistant a top priority for the remainder of the summer and throughout the school year. For instance, the directing principal discusses the contract-mandated staff evaluation protocols. The assistant explains the district behavior management policy and how it is implemented.

After school starts, before the new assistant goes off to central office for his first student-services hearing, the assistant explains the hearing process to him: what materials to bring, the sequence of events in such hearings, how to prepare for his comments in the hearing, who would attend the hearing—in short, everything he needs to know in order to participate effectively in the hearing. To finish the example, the directing principal and both assistant principals do a "How did it go?" debrief afterward.

"Listen to Me" works well as a stand-alone mentoring process. However, in more cases than not "Listen to Me" serves as the stepping-off point of the mentoring process.

The fourth mentoring level is "Walk with Me." In this situation, the supervisor brings the new employee along as he works at a task for which the new employee will have similar responsibility. In just about all cases, "Walk with Me" follows an introductory "Listen to Me" situation. The complete mentoring session should end with a debriefing session.

As an example, "Walk with Me" works well when orienting new administrators to the IEP process. The new administrator sits in, as an observer, in school support team meetings, meetings which determine whether or not a student qualifies for special education services, and IEP development meetings. This gives the new principal experience with the processes, enabling effective participation when he or she is an active participant.

"Work with Me" is the fifth level of mentoring. The new employee learns a process by working with the supervisor, who is the school expert. An example of this is the whole administrative team, including the new assistant, working on the design of the master schedule for the coming year. Prior to becoming the official scheduler the new assistant gets hands-on experience with each phase of the scheduling process.

The educational leader must anticipate all situations for which a new employee needs mentorship. The educational leader designs the type of mentorship appropriate for each situation.

The mentor (often the same person) commits to and provides mentorship at the appropriate time.

HIERARCHY OF MENTORSHIP—ACTIVITY

Using one or more of the mentoring processes outlined in this chapter, develop a full mentoring program that reflects the needs and resources available in your school/district.

HIERARCHY OF MENTORSHIP—REFLECTION

Identify mentoring situations in which each of the mentoring processes would work best for you. Take into consideration the task at hand, how you learn, and which mentoring approach would best fit each.

2

Professional Goal Setting

AREAS OF FOCUS

This chapter is focused on you and your role as an administrator. Typically, people who are chosen for an administrative position have both the knowledge and experience to create some pretty impressive credentials. So now you've secured an administrative position and the question becomes, "Where do I go from here?"

There are several areas on which goals can focus:

- relational: Who do you need to get to know better? What is your relationship with parents, staff, students, other administrators, board members, and community members?
- attitude: Are there any behaviors that you wish to focus on with which you are not currently happy? Is there any part of your mindset holding you back? In the words of Eleanor Roosevelt, "No one can make you feel inferior without your consent" (*This Is My Story*, 1937).
- career: How far do you want to go? What are you willing to do to get there? How long do you think it will take you to get to where you want to be? How will this goal help you advance in your career? Will it make you more marketable, or can it hinder your chances for advancement?
- education: Are there additional degrees or licenses you need to obtain to advance or keep your current credentials active? Is there another area that interests you?
- financial: Are you happy with your current salary and benefits? Are you in a position where someone advocates for you? Is there room for advancement, or might you need to change positions in order to experience an increase? If you move within a district, will they compensate you accordingly or would they bring in an external candidate at a higher salary?

- enjoyment: Do you like your job? If not, what can be put in place for you to find joy in going to work each day? If so, what are the best parts that can be shared with others?
- service: How do you share your gifts and talents with others? Do you search for opportunities to assist in the community? Do you have a student council, Scouts, or other groups with whom you can work to model to all students the importance of involvement in your community?

In reality, your journey continues and the question is really, "Where do you want to go from here?" The beauty of goals is that they are always changing. Goals may change due to completion, refocusing, reconsideration, changes within one's personal life, or opportunities that have presented themselves.

GUIDELINES FOR GOAL SETTING

Identifying goals has a number of purposes.

First, goals focus us. Instead of scattered ideas, we have our eye on the prize. Interests and effort are channeled with an end mean in sight. Goals have two primary attributes: content and intensity (Locke and Latham, 1990). Goal content refers to the features of the goals themselves (e.g., the difficulty and specificity of the goal). Goal intensity is the process by which a goal is set and accomplished (Lee, Locke, and Latham, 1989; Locke and Latham, 1990). It relates to factors such as individual commitment, and the cognitive processes involved in attaining and setting goals. (Yearta, Maitlis, and Briner, 1995).

Second, goals energize us. More difficult goals take greater effort, but if we have known goals and a plan in place, we are more apt to make the goals a reality. In an infamous study done by Yale University (as cited in Locke, Shaw, Saari, & Latham, 1981) the 3 percent of the graduating class who had known goals demonstrated greater measureable success, including higher wages and positions, than the other 97 percent of the class who did not have known goals. Laboratory and field studies involving specific and challenging goals led to higher performance than easy or absent goals (Locke et al., 1981).

Goal setting is a process where self-evaluation of where you are and where you want to be in life helps to focus and give direction. As one proceeds there is a sense of pride and accomplishment, self-confidence, and recognition of competence and abilities (MindTools, 2010).

Third, goals call for persistence. The person makes a conscious decision to dedicate time, energy, and finances to successfully complete the goal. It is one thing to dream a dream; it is another to invest in it, keep focused, and successfully complete it.

It is important to keep in mind that goals are not stringent, but should be reviewed and re-evaluated on a regular basis. This review offers the opportune time to revise or even scrap a goal. If a goal is scrapped, question why you have made that decision as well as whether or not to replace that goal with another.

Keep in mind the difference between wants and needs. For example, you may need to take courses or credit hours to keep your license current; or you may want to take a course because it is an area that interests you. Goals that reflect wants may be the first to be changed or cut altogether, whereas goals that reflect needs require accommodations be made to ensure these are successfully completed.

A person should have both short-term and long-term goals and should keep the number of goals to ones that allow you to maintain focus. Being overzealous can cause you to feel overwhelmed. It is better to finish a goal and have a sense of accomplishment and then go on to another than to have a laundry list of goals where you don't complete any and feel like you've failed.

There may be some goals that have to be done in a pretty short time frame, such as when we begin a new position and there is the learning curve affiliated with learning the new position. Examples are learning the names of staff, parents, and students, or learning new software that the district uses. Then there are long-term goals, such as obtaining additional licensure or the next level of education.

Goals need to be specific. By doing this you have set your sites on a specific set of tasks that calls for a certain type of behavior on your part. Rather than allow for a wide range of acceptable performance levels, you focus in on what it is you actually want. Making a statement that you want to be rich is different than having a goal of being a millionaire by the time you are forty.

Find a support system. Look at each goal individually and determine who can help you meet that goal. Who offers words of encouragement? Who can help with resources necessary for you to meet that goal? Who's your go-to person to help you problem solve? Who's been through this or something like it where they understand? Are you taking on additional or new duties at the workplace that comfortably allow you to work on these goals? Are you setting yourself up for failure or success? How will you work through stress? Who can help you measure your progression, and who can assist you with prioritizing your goals into manageable segments?

Find a way to hold yourself accountable. Be sure your goals are based on you and what you can do to reach them. You don't want to rely on other people for your success. While goals can be aligned with the direction of personal or district goals, they must be your goals and meaningful to you. Imposed goals offer no buy-in unless, perhaps, there is a monetary prize upon completion. Ask yourself why this is a goal, and whether or not you believe you can actually attain it. Life is about balance. Have a manageable number of goals that reflect your desires. Focus on the outcome, not the challenges to get there.

Celebrate accomplishments. If you complete a goal, share it with your staff, parents, students, and community. Do the same for others. Whether it is completion of a degree, additional licensure, publication of an article, or being the recipient of an award, you have risen to the challenge and that is cause to celebrate.

GOAL SETTING—ACTIVITY

Brainstorm some ideas to assist with your goal writing. What would you like to see for yourself both short term (one to five years) and long term (five to ten years)? Which areas would you like to focus on: relational, attitude, career, education, financial, enjoyment, or service?

Put your list aside for a few days.
Review your list. What stands out to you? Create a list of three short-term and three long-term goals. Write them in a positive manner as though you have accomplished them already.

Short Term (one to five years)

Long Term (five to ten years)

Add to each goal: (1) a timeline for when that goal will be complete, and (2) who can assist and support you as you work to reach each goal.

REFLECTION—GOAL SETTING

How did you feel as you were thinking about goal setting? Were you apprehensive, put out, excited, hesitant, looking for a challenge . . . ?

Are you ready to commit to the goals that you have set for yourself?

Do you have a plan in place that includes timelines and support?

How do you think these goals can and will change your life?

How do you think you will handle the situation if you don't meet a goal? Will you rewrite the goal, come up with an alternate plan . . . ?

What is your motivation to complete these goals? Are you externally motivated by money, title, and material items, or intrinsically motivated with a sense of accomplishment? Will you find contentment with completion of these goals?

How are you going to take a pulse on your goals?

3

Leadership Evaluation Tool

The following rating scale is to be used quarterly throughout the first year in a new administrative position, with the recommendation to participate in mentoring for the first three years in a new position. The Educational Leadership Mentoring/Coaching Evaluation Tool was developed after analyzing State Administrator Standards from various states. The tool helps to recognize competencies and strengths, identify areas of weakness, and address areas where the user may not have had much experience.

This tool also allows the district to identify skills or areas of priority for the new educational leader. As with teachers, mentors/coaches should practice public praise and private criticisms or corrections. Hope; encouragement; and positive, constructive, specific feedback are imperative to the success of the educational leader.

Ratings are as follows:

Not **E**vident: The leader has not demonstrated skills and/or knowledge in this area, or knowledge and skills are of poor quality.
Basic: The leader demonstrates a combination of high and low quality of knowledge and skills and/or minimal evidence.
Proficient: The leader consistently demonstrates high-quality knowledge and skills with satisfactory evidence of use.
Distinguished: The leader exemplifies exceptional knowledge and consistent, high-quality skills with clear evidence.

Table 3.1. Administrative Standards

Leadership	NE	B	P	D
Demonstrates competence as a leader and an educator				
Creates and makes known the mission, vision, and goals of the school				
Ability to develop and monitor a strategic plan				
Establishes benchmarks, expectations, and feedback measures to ensure accountability				
Leader of, but member of, a team				
Distributes leadership, shares responsibilities, and demonstrates a collaborative nature				
Recruits, trains, supports, and retains highly competent personnel				
Coaches for improvement				
Is accessible, approachable, and engaged in the school community				
Supports and articulates major initiatives and change efforts				
Supports innovative thinking and risk-taking efforts				
Encourages and inspires others to higher levels of commitment, performance, and motivation				
Understands and participates in conflict management				
Balances personal and professional responsibilities				
Reflection of understanding sound, research-based theories and techniques of classroom management, student discipline, and school safety				
Instruction and Learning	NE	B	P	D
Advocates, nurtures, and sustains school culture				
Maximizes student achievement				
Teachers are mentored/coached for student success				
Professional development of faculty/staff that demonstrate research-based and best practice strategies				
Instruction is differentiated/adapted for the success of all				
There is equity and accessibility to curriculum and resources				
Effective use of multiple resources				
High expectations for all				
Equity, fairness, and respect are mutual				
Recognition of students as active learners				
Supports instruction that is engaging, rigorous, relevant and offers choices to the students				
Assessments reflect and complement instructional practices				
Student progress is reported in a manner that aligns with skills assessed				
Facilitates design and implementation of curricula and a strategic plan that enhance teaching and learning with ongoing monitoring and revision				

(*continued*)

Table 3.1. (*continued*)

Technology is integrated				
Speakers and other opportunities are utilized				
Extracurricular experiences that reflect the needs and desire of the community are offered				
Reflection and inquiry are valued				
Focuses on quality over quantity of curriculum				
Continual assessment focused on individual improvement and academic performance; focus on proficiency levels over grade levels				
Data-Driven Decision Making	NE	B	P	D
Successfully access, manipulate, and analyze multiple sources of data				
Establishes metrics, collect and analyze data, interpret results to improve staff performance and student learning				
Demonstrates understanding of research and/or best practices to improve educational programming				
Shared Vision	NE	B	P	D
The vision of the school is developed, articulated, and implemented				
The vision reflects multiple measures of student learning and relevant quality indicators				
Identifies and addresses barriers				
Shapes school programs, plans, and activities to be consistent with vision				
Builds environment conducive to realization of vision				
Promotes innovation				
Shared with and supported by community				
Alignment of fiscal, human, and material resources				
Sustains safe, efficient, well-maintained, and productive school environment				
Behavior management reflects effective and nurturing practices				
Ongoing evaluation of programs and staff				
Use of issues, trends, demographic data, knowledge of systems, campus climate inventories, and student learning data to plan and implement vision				
Collaboration	NE	B	P	D
Responsive to needs				
Builds relationship with families and community members				
Builds home and school communication				
Mobilizes community resources such as health and social services				
Incorporates family/community information in decision making				

(*continued*)

Table 3.1. (*continued*)

Communication	NE	B	P	D
Effective verbal, nonverbal, and written communication				
Articulates programs				
Generates support for the school				
Encourages constructive conversations about improvement of student learning and achievement				
Communicates vertically *and* horizontally				
Communication is ongoing				
Reflects the needs of the community (i.e., offered in other languages)				
Progress of goals is communicated				
Systematically and fairly recognizes and celebrates accomplishments of staff and students				
Group consensus				
Effectively uses media				
Teachers have been informed as to how they will be evaluated, including observations, self-report forms, checklists, appraisals, or other forms of review				
Teachers have all necessary materials for reviews, including a calendar of visitation, forms, policies, improvement plans, appeal process, grievances, etc.				
Teachers have received an orientation including performance appraisal system information with a copy of the instrument used				
Defines roles, assigns functions, delegates authority, and determines accountability toward goals				
Frames, analyzes, and creatively resolves problems				
Professional Practice	NE	B	P	D
Fiscal and time commitments to professional development				
Provides both in- and out-of-district opportunities				
Administrator/s and teachers have input through needs, interests, reflection of strengths/weaknesses, and development of programs				
Professional goals of teachers and administrators are written and reflected upon				
Provides opportunities in alignment with identified goals of the district				
Collaboratively develops, implements, and revises comprehensive and ongoing professional development plan				
Promotes knowledge and skills and models lifelong learning				
Social, Legal, and Ethical	NE	B	P	D
Displays integrity, fairness, and honesty				
Displays respect				

(*continued*)

Table 3.1. (continued)	NE	B	P	D
Acts in a professional manner				
Works within the parameters of federal, state, and local laws, policies, regulations, and statutes				
Works well with governing board				
Works for educational, not personal gain				
Displays an understanding of politics, economics, ethics, and justice				
Demonstrates an understanding of the cultural context of the district				
Displays understanding of district policy, privacy, security, online safety, and acceptable use				
Displays understanding of copyrights and intellectual property				
Understands and manages legal and contractual agreements				
Maintains accurate records				
Is respectful and open to all opinions				
Builds a caring relationship with faculty and staff				
Inspires others through values, beliefs, and attitudes displayed				

Areas of strength for this educational leader are:

Areas of growth identified include:

Area/s of improvement to address during the school year:

List some accomplishments from this quarter of which you are most proud:

Signature of Educational Leader: _____   Date: _____

Signature of Mentor/Coach: _____   Date: _____

Title/Position: _____

Record of Review:

Review of the assessment instrument should include both the leader and mentor as active participants. This review may include discussion of challenges and progress, review and rewriting of goals, and determination of the areas to focus on during the next quarter.

Quarter 1 date _____   Quarter 2 date _____

Quarter 3 date _____   Quarter 4 date _____

4

Professional Standards, Personal Life

The topic of behavior in a public position is not new. One can look at Rules for Teachers in 1872 to view the expectations of the times. Though they may seem questionable to us, they were a way of life during the time of inception:

1. Teachers each day will fill lamps, clean chimneys.
2. Each teacher will bring a bucket of water and a scuttle of coal for the day's session.
3. Make your pens carefully. You may whittle nibs to the individual taste of the pupils.
4. Men teachers may take one evening each week for courting purposes, or two evenings a week if they go to church regularly.
5. After ten hours in school, the teachers may spend the remaining time reading the Bible or other good books.
6. Women teachers who marry or engage in unseemly conduct will be dismissed.
7. Every teacher should lay aside from each pay a goodly sum of his earnings for his benefit during his declining years so that he will not become a burden on society.
8. Any teacher who smokes, uses liquor in any form, frequents pool or public halls, or gets shaved in a barber shop will give good reason to suspect his worth, intention, integrity, and honesty.
9. The teacher who performs his labor fruitfully and without fault for five years will be given an increase of twenty-five cents per week in his pay, providing the Board of Education approves.

Though times have changed, the following question begs an answer as it flies in the face of contemporary culture. The question needs to be addressed if all of us working in the field of education take education and our role in it seriously. Should an educational leader set standards for his or her own personal life?

The question calls for definition of the very subjective terms "educational leader," "standards," and "personal life." "Educational leader" in terms of the context of the present work refers to principals and assistant principals—people who supervise and work with teachers, support staff, and students in a school setting. "Standards" in this context refers to principles which govern behavior. And "personal life" is that part of an educational leader's experience outside of work responsibilities—that life that exists outside of the school day, away from students and staff.

To simplify the question: Should a school principal live by standards outside of the school setting which reflect ethical behavior in the school setting? The answer, absolutely, is yes.

The argument heard over and over again promotes just the opposite: No, a school principal should apply standards of ethical behavior in the school setting, but what a school principal does in his or her personal life has nothing to do with work. Personal life is personal life. No one has any business commenting on personal life.

In other words, if an educational leader has set a low bar for personal standards, it does not conflict with the high bar he has set for professional standards. The two sets of standards do not have to be compatible. The educational leader acts one way in the job and another way in the personal life; the two have nothing to do with one another. In terms of educational leadership and mentoring, does one have the right to even ask such a question?

This is an area of controversy. If a school administrator is appropriate in all school behaviors, all interactions with staff, parents, and students; but leads a sordid life after school hours by chasing women, drinking excessively, using illegal drugs, so what?

The administrator's boss evaluates him in terms of his effectiveness in meeting district expectations. His staff knows him as a person with a high degree of professionalism and behavior. So do the students. So do the parents. So does central administration. The question is, "What educator can lead a personal life entirely separate and different from the professional life?"

The sad reality is the truth will come out. If a school administrator is fooling around, people will find out about it and will talk about it. A secret life remains secret only so long. Once the secret is out, it's out. What happens then to the image of the administrator? What happens to the respect the administrator may have had? What happens to the administrator's effectiveness?

The point of contention is school administrators should not live two lives. Any school administrator who has a problem with that should seriously consider finding a different job, where behavior outside of work does not matter.

Leadership with this issue is simple: Lead by example. Let your own standards of personal and professional behavior be an inspiration to all personnel in your school, including those administrators who work for you.

Mentoring with this issue is simple. When working with a new administrator, establish the ground rules. If necessary, state expectations for appropriate behaviors in the school setting as well as out of it. Make sure your subordinates understand the concept.

PERSONAL LIFE—ACTIVITY

Outline the conversation you should have with your mentor as a new administrator. Be sure to identify expectations of the district/school for you as an administrator, as well as expectations of those whom you will lead and supervise.

PERSONAL LIFE—REFLECTION

Evaluate your personal life.
Identify the components of your life that are representative of positive role modeling.

Is there discord between the life you live at school and the life you live outside of school? If so, identify aspects of your personal life that you should change to live the life that you want your students, parents, and staff to think that you live.

5

Defining Leadership

UNDERSTANDING LEADERSHIP

There is a difference between leadership and management. All managers are not leaders and all leaders are not managers. With this in mind, let's first look at what is meant by educational leadership and management.

Educational leadership incorporates attributes such as: goal setting; teamwork and collaboration; support; listening; communicating; development, articulation, implementation, and execution of a common vision; motivating; risk taking; inspiring; moving people toward their goals; and capitalizing on the strengths of each individual as part of the whole of the team.

A manager plans, controls, directs; hires carefully and is not afraid to fire; creates a (financially) productive environment; communicates; coaches; builds morale; takes on projects; is a decision maker; and focuses on customer service. While many of the attributes may be similar, it is the approach that defines a leader from a manager.

A good leader understands that she or he earns the right to be responsible for others through integrity and building trusting and respectful relationships. It is the ability to lead others that truly separates a leader from a manager.

In a session with astronaut Col. Eileen Collins, several insights of leadership were shared (Collins, 2009). Three characteristics of leaders are knowledge of your job, working well with people, and display of integrity. One must have technical knowledge, meaning you know your people well: talents, interests, and family needs. One needs to communicate. One must display integrity, meaning that you trust that person will be honest in the future and has standards, no personal gains are involved in decision making, and decisions are made for the good of all.

Cultural issues, basic norms, beliefs, and practices at the basic level define how we do them. We need to be better listeners, more humble and creative. To be a better listener, display an open mind, participate in active listening, and ask people what they think.

Display confidence but a willingness to give other people's ideas a chance. Think hard—maybe there's something that can be done. Think outside the box, even on daily doings. Be innovative and creative. On a daily basis ask, "What can make us fail?"

Find techniques to lower stress. A leader needs to be respected but not liked. Be spontaneous. You make the future. Brainstorm for input. Generate conflict for creativity, and keep in mind that all ideas are important.

LEADERSHIP STYLES

The terminology that describes leadership styles is not a definitive one. Depending on the author, different terms are used. Some of the terms you may come across include authoritative, democratic, autocratic, paternalistic, laissez-faire, coach, permissive, collaborative, and directive. Some of these terms have a negative connotation, such as authoritarian, because an employee does not want to work under authority. It is the same on the other end of the spectrum in that employees don't like to work for someone permissive because they usually can't make a decision.

Therefore, it is important for leaders to not only take into consideration the spectrum and where you fall, but also the situation and work environment. For example, perhaps your school has specific rules, as noted in your handbook, regarding bereavement days. An employee comes to you upset because she just found out her aunt died. This aunt didn't raise her, but was very close to her. The aunt didn't have children of her own and treated your employee as her own child. You have a choice in how you handle the situation.

Regarding work environment, let's say an employee comes to you and asks to take a sick day to go fishing. Initial response: "What? Yeah, right." Consider that the person works in an alternative school or is in a special education placement. You know burnout is high. The day would be a stress reliever, and your employee may return refocused and rejuvenated. What do you say?

Consider the sayings, such as people join companies and leave managers, or that managers think people leave because of salaries and benefits when in fact people leave because of lack of appreciation by those very managers.

A great leader listens to ideas, concerns, questions, and information. The employee is heard in his or her entirety. All is taken into account before a decision is made. A great leader will recognize the efforts and accomplishments of the employee. You know your employee always comes early and leaves late. Willingness to let her leave a little early for a doctor appointment or run to pick up a sick child during the day goes a long way. You build a relationship of trust and respect.

Your employee should never have to guess what you want. Expectations should be clear, shared, and discussed more than just at the time of appraisal. A great leader assists his or her staff in reaching professional goals, even if it means that they have their sights set on a job of equal or higher title. Finally, if your staff can perform without you being present, you have developed outstanding employees and demonstrated great leadership.

Grzeskowiak (2010) states, "Good teachers will recognize that not all students have the same learning style, and will adjust their teaching style accordingly. The same can be said for management styles—not all employees function well under one style, and good managers will vary their style according to personality types and practical needs."

TWENTY-FIRST-CENTURY LEADERSHIP STYLES

Today's educational leaders need a different skill set than past generations. In *Primal Leadership*, Goleman, Boyatzis, and McKee (2002) identified six styles of leadership listed in order of preference from most effective to least:

- Visionary—the leader creates a vision that engages people to buy in and share the dream. Engaged employees give more effort and higher performance and have less turnover. Engaged employees are inspired by confident and connected leaders.
- Coaching—the leader connects individual needs and wants with organizational goals.
- Affiliative—the leader connects people, creating teamwork. The collaborative approach builds relationships that impact performance, loyalty, and commitment.
- Democratic—the leader recognizes each group member's value and seeks to include each member, and has active participation from each. Everyone in the group has leadership potential and can play leadership roles at various times. If consensus cannot be reached, the leader makes the decision.
- Pacesetting—the leader sets and achieves goals, promoting self over the good of all.
- Commanding—the leader provides clear direction and makes all decisions.

You don't have to be an expert to be a good leader. An expert is a go-to person concerning job tasks. A leader provides direction and motivation in order to achieve goals. The twenty-first-century skills are more focused on ingenuity, rapport, and gut instinct than on knowledge in and of itself. Leaders of today balance logic and vision; speaking and listening; predictability and spontaneity; making and breaking the rules; process and people; criticism and forgiveness; and leading with their head vs. their heart (Juech, 2009).

Good leaders are willing and able to change. They manage and inspire, and welcome candid feedback that may invite the hard truth, but provide direction to overcome some areas in need of improvement.

Leadership is about two things: relationships and results. If you help others reach their goals, listen and keep an open mind, freely implement other people's ideas, allow others to look good, and give credit where credit is due, you will be known as a selfless leader focused on the good of all over the good of one. General Colin Powell said, "There's no end to what you can accomplish if you don't care who gets the credit."

RELEVANCY OF TWENTY-FIRST-CENTURY LEADERSHIP SKILLS

Information is to be fresh, concise, and relevant. Information is to be chunked so new administrators have what they need to succeed. There are certain skills recognized as building blocks for confident leaders. These include:

- Personal/Professional Growth Management Skills: self-assessment and the willingness to commit to financial, energy, and time requirements to determine the quality and successful completion of personal and professional goals.
- Communication and Connection Skills: How skillfully a leader communicates is a major factor of credibility. Communication must be consistent and credible. One must confidently confront issues and create a safe environment for discussion. Honest and open communication builds trust—a foremost requirement for leaders. Communication includes listening to understand, reflecting on other's opinions, open-mindedness, and searching for common ground amid diversity.
- Messaging Skills: Desire and intent is very important to those you lead. Create and articulate a clear vision.
- Networking Skills: Network with colleagues and those with connections to your position. Through improved connectivity, one can make the most of people's knowledge and work across boundaries. Networking builds collaboration and community.

- Giving Skills: Help others, both individually and within the community, and you will find that you grow. Promoting the development of others is obtained through leaders' modeling, inspiring, teaching, delegating, and serving.
- Collective Facilitations Skills: Design and facilitate effective meetings. Focusing collective energy toward a shared vision calls for commitment to the process, dedication to the welfare of the group, and detachment from the need to hold power and control others. This means the group develops or obtains the resources necessary to achieve its goals. This process is based on respect, encouragement, and community building.
- Storytelling Skills: Engage others in the connection between understanding and action.

Leaders of the twenty-first century motivate, empower, articulate, and innovate. While twenty-first-century leaders acknowledge that leadership still means showing people the way, they share leadership. Attitudes and behaviors of the leader determine the context in which others will act.

DEFINING LEADERSHIP—ACTIVITY

Get to know your leadership style. Take a look at the following websites. Each looks at management or leadership in a different way.

    www.queendom.com/queendom_tests/transfer
    www.yourleadershiplegacy.com/assessment/assessment.php
    www.thetrustedleader.com
    www.leadership-with-you.com/DISC-personality-test.html

Look carefully at your results. While the assessments use different terminology, what leadership qualities stand out to you as strengths? Were there any areas that stood out to you as needing attention? How can you incorporate these results into your current position?

DEFINING LEADERSHIP—REFLECTION

Think about administrators you have known in the past, whether you were a student, subordinate, or peer. What leadership qualities did they characterize that made them quality administrators?

Based on the descriptions given above, what were your observations of how others interacted with the administrators?

What are some ways you could implement these observations into your own environment?

6

Mentoring the Leader

It is important to understand one's leadership style so you can approach mentoring in a way that will be effective for that person. Just as each of us has our own teaching, learning, thinking, or parenting style, we each have our own leadership and mentoring style. As we become seasoned parents, we realize we need to make adjustments and take individuality into account in our approach to discipline, tough conversations, enforcement of rules, or completion of projects. So it is with understanding one's leadership style and approach to mentoring in a way that will prove effective for each mentee as an individual.

MENTORING STYLES

Depending on the research, styles of mentoring can be addressed through different names; however, the approaches are similar in nature regardless of what they are called.

The direct or unidirectional approach to mentoring offers professional direction grounded in veteran knowledge and experience. Technical advice is often provided comfortably as the mentor has the background to openly share experience.

The guided collaboration or collaborative approach defines the mentor and mentee as colleagues and peers. The mentor is not viewed as an expert per se, but a colleague to run one's ideas by. This approach combines mentor facilitation with mentee exploration. Problem solving takes place through sharing in open discussions.

The nondirective or reciprocal approach is where the mentor believes that the mentee will seek them out if there are questions; thus, the mentor supports the mentee's autonomy and understanding of one's self while the mentor shares in his or her development. This is more of a hands-off, use-as-needed approach. The mentee knows where to go if questions arise, but has the autonomy to continue work as usual with his or her own way of problem solving. The mentor is more of a voice in the head and may listen or encourage if asked his or her opinion or insight.

THE MENTORING PROCESS

The mentoring program should span three years: two full years of direct support and one year of maintenance. An on-site mentor is often the most effective, since conversations can be informal, spontaneous, and on the spot. However, as a mentor is matched with a mentee, one must consider a number of variables, including match between positions' duties and responsibilities, availability, load, and connections.

The match between the mentor and mentee's duties and responsibilities should be at least close enough where the mentor can actually give some insight as to how they've handled responsibilities. For example, if you have an excellent curriculum director, but the person has not served as a school principal, there is probably a better match with someone who handles more similar responsibilities, such as student discipline and irate parents.

While it is best to have a mentor from within the same district so there is a familiarity of philosophy, resources, policies, procedures, student management systems, and so forth, the size of the district, number of administrators, and types of administrators may call for there to be partnerships between local districts to share resources and more closely match roles.

Availability and load are directly related in that you want to offer a mentor who is not too wrapped up in projects of his or her own. If she or he is trying to meet deadlines, the mentee becomes another project, a nuisance or an inconvenience rather than someone to walk beside. Time management must be practiced on both sides, and specific time set aside for both in order to connect, catch up, discuss, throw out questions, and such will not take place without some effort.

Search for connections when matching mentors and mentees. Preferences of mentoring or learning styles, and outside interests such as specific sports, teams, or crafts can serve as core to building a solid mentor-mentee relationship. Connections between the two, such as a mutual friend, their children playing on the same soccer team, or attending the same church, can also serve as a starting point to build a trusting relationship. If there is no trust, there are limits to the sharing and the mentoring will not be effective.

Following are some essentials to an effective mentoring program:

- Offer ongoing, nonjudgmental direct support. As a veteran administrator, remember: they don't know what you do. That came with experience. Provide training, professional development, resources, and support needed for success.

- Discuss expectations, and provide strong examples of them. Hold the mentee accountable to the desired level of performance.
- Go beyond providing feedback. Describe what needs adjustment, give clear examples of how those adjustments can be made, and then follow through by providing support, targeted professional development, or observations and/or pairing with veterans in similar roles.
- Have defined meeting times for the mentor and mentee to meet, and make the meeting a priority. By maintaining an ongoing pulse of the progress, challenges, and accomplishments, you can increase the likelihood of retention of your administrator. Communication between the mentor and mentee should be regular and accessible. The participants should have cell numbers, e-mails, or other information to ensure contact can be made. Make training available to point the mentee to success. For example, student management software used by the school or district may call for training, a guide on the side during the first uses, and technical support.
- Understand the needs of the mentee. Remember that we all had a first year in our position. Mistakes should not be viewed as fatal, but as learning experiences. There are no stupid questions.
- Modify your program for those who enter mid-year. Jump them in. Determine what they need to know right away, and what you can share later. Just don't forget that they need support, perhaps even more by starting mid-year.
- Evaluation of the program is a necessity. What worked, what didn't, and what could be done better in the future to meet the needs of new administrators? What was the person's accessibility? Were responses offered, and in a timely manner? Is additional or more thorough training necessary in specific areas, and what areas would these be? Questions should be asked from both mentor and mentee perspective. If these questions are not asked, and thoughtfully answered, the program remains stagnant and ineffective.
- Be prepared to handle situations, as there may be different issues for someone promoted internally versus someone brought in externally. With an established relationship with the staff, there may be some in support of the move to administration, while others may question or be vocal about the move in a negative way. The transition from peer to supervisor may also be cause for discussion.

FORTY THINGS YOU CAN DO WITH YOUR MENTEE

- Remind the mentee of important deadlines (e.g., state paperwork).
- Assist with completion of forms, or direct the mentee to resources to do so.
- Introduce the administrator to area administrators, particularly with similar roles.

- Assist the administrator with networking.
- Set time aside to touch base on a regular basis.
- Be accessible, including if your mentee needs you spontaneously.
- Invite your mentee to lunch.
- Offer assistance with student management software and other district programs.
- Discuss behavior management in the district.
- Introduce mentee to key people: board members, parents, community members, and so on.
- Listen attentively to the concerns and frustrations of the mentee; determine whether or not the mentee actually wants advice.
- Offer guidance with planning events the first year.
- Share traditions of the school and community.
- Attend a workshop or conference with the mentee.
- Advise mentee on personnel issues.
- Provide a confidential setting.
- Provide specific feedback including any self-defeating behaviors.
- Invite the mentee to an off-campus social event outside of business hours.
- Introduce the mentee to resource persons within the district.
- Provide counsel on conflict resolution matters.
- Encourage participation in professional organizations.
- Patiently answer questions.
- Model professionalism.
- Discuss high expectations of the district and ways to meet these expectations.
- Share a sense of humor.
- Discuss educational issues and trends.
- Share a sense of appreciation for those in administrative positions.
- Share a compliment about your mentee with a colleague, in front of your mentee.
- Discuss a plan toward professional growth.
- Share your own challenges and successes.
- Be cognizant of the mentee's state of being throughout the year: elation, coping, survival.
- Assist with time management.
- Share district policies and procedures.
- Share in brainstorming sessions to problem solve.
- Keep abreast in the field, and openly discuss topics.
- Establish an open, honest relationship.
- Communicate clearly and often.
- Discuss student issues: academic, behavior, parent communication, and so on.
- Build trust.
- Accept and assist the mentee, regardless of "friend" status.

MENTORING THE LEADER—ACTIVITY

Reread the leadership styles in the previous chapter. Then reread the mentoring styles in this chapter. Which styles do you feel would be most effective coupled together?

Go back into the chapter and read the section on mentoring styles. Which style do you feel you would work best with, and why?

What information could you share with your mentor to establish trust? Create a more effective mentor-mentee relationship? Make your experience together a positive one?

List some activities that you would look forward to participating in with your mentor.

36   *Chapter 6*

MENTORING THE LEADER—REFLECTION

Sometimes we are our own worst enemy. With high expectations, many duties assigned, wearing several hats, full schedules, and shrinking hours in a day, we put a lot of pressure on ourselves as leaders. Below are some false statements. Reflect on them and what they mean to you, and list some ways your mentor can assist.

Strong leadership means that I can do it myself.

Strong leadership means I don't need to ask for help.

Strong leadership means that I know all of the answers.

Strong leadership means that I listen to the problem and solve it for you.

Strong leadership means that the decision making is left to me.

Strong leadership means that I will not make mistakes.

7

Understanding School Culture

Every school has its own culture, even if there are multiple schools within the same district. In a series called *Through New Eyes* (Fullan, 2003), culture over structure is discussed. Structure means programs, procedures, policies, and rules. Culture means assumptions, expectations, beliefs, and habits that constitute norms that drive daily ways. The culture provides meaning and stability, and reculturing leads to more effective restructuring. The culture of any school can be found in the assumptions we don't see.

STAFF

A collaborative culture has all staff working together for the success of every student. Build a culture where continuous improvement is practiced. To promote a collaborative environment, certain pieces must be in place.

First, there must be trust. If teachers feel that what they share becomes public, judged, or the center of competition, chances are that you have lost the opportunity to maintain collaboration and relationships need to be rebuilt before you can continue.

Second is confidentiality. If staff is sharing with you as their leader, it is based on trust. Compromising that trust by sharing confidential information can be devastating to a relationship, both personal and professional.

Third is professionalism. Maintaining professionalism means your attire speaks of your position; your mouth is not spewing curse words; you act as a role model for your staff; and your actions show that you not only talk the talk, but walk the walk. It also means that you share and enforce expectations on your staff. In other words, in your district do you allow miniskirts and flip-flops as teaching attire? If you have a teacher who yells at students all of the time, is that acceptable?

The fourth area is knowing and understanding boundaries. The obvious here is not putting yourself in any predicaments with students, parents, or colleagues that could be misconstrued or questioned.

Boundaries also include cell phone usage. During a meeting, turn the cell phone off. When talking to someone, turn it off or don't answer it. Don't stand there texting while someone is talking to you. Instead, give people your undivided attention. Make them feel that they are important enough for you to stop what you are doing and give them your time. Being in the moment and attentive to the person's needs goes a long way. By modeling this behavior, you are creating a culture that demonstrates people first.

ENVIRONMENT

The environment really sets the tone for students. We live in a society where sometimes we take things for granted; unfortunately, third world countries and some of our schools here in the United States have parallels. For example, running water, having toilet paper available, open food or containers where extra milk is discarded that is left for hours and has flies buzzing around may seem unreal to some of us, but it is a reality. Burnt-out lights, ripped carpeting, graffiti on the walls, and overflowing wastebaskets are easy fixes that can bring an environment from unacceptable to tolerable.

Look for ways to increase the positive feelings that can be stimulated, such as live plants, colorful displays that are changed on a regular basis, order, and routine. Search for ways to address noise levels. This is not necessarily the noise level within a classroom, but outside noises that could distract students' learning. For example, in one school there is a man who drums all afternoon. While his students may like to hear the names of the states and their capitals drummed out, there are classrooms on each side of his. Classrooms close to the cafeteria or gymnasium may prove to be challenged.

With schools stretched for space, classrooms end up in created spaces, like hallways, shower rooms, coat rooms, and closets. This can cause problems not only for noise, but also for temperature. A created classroom in a hallway can prove to be cold in the northern territory during winter months and difficult to heat. A classroom in a closet that is not ventilated well and has a bunch of little bodies in it can go from warm to hot very quickly. Add some computers and the heat level rises further.

TRADITIONS

It is often the parents or community members over the students who anticipate, require, and support traditions. These traditions may be special days celebrated during the school year that commemorate a community or school event.

It may be the way that a celebration takes place, such as graduation. Perhaps it's holding certain community fund-raisers, like a fish boil, turkey dinner, or silent auction. It may be an anticipated field trip in a specific grade level, like a trip to Washington, D.C., or annual assignments given by the same teacher each year, like a living museum. Regardless, these traditions have become rooted within the culture of the school. Parents anticipate them. Students anticipate them. Change them and it most likely will not be a popular decision.

EXPECTATIONS

The expectations of the board, community members, parents, staff, students, and administration all come into play. The expectations must be clear, concise, and communicated. At all levels, the expectations must be taught, consistent, and enforced. If there is deviation from these expectations, then one is to be held accountable. It should be brought to the attention of the person along with specific feedback of what does not fit as well as possibilities to correct the situation. Joint problem solving, listening, interaction, coaching, mentoring, and ongoing communication are of great importance for a school to run cohesively and in unity.

DIVERSITY

There are many ways a school can prove to be diverse. Having all to most of one ethnic group, regardless of the group represented, does not show diversity. A true mix of ethnic backgrounds is one way to show diversity.

Another way is through programs offered, such as athletics, band, theatre, forensics, and chess. Having programs in your school that focus on hearing impaired, wheelchair bound, ELL, Gifted and Talented, and such demonstrates variation and provides students a true opportunity to work with other students who may have backgrounds different than their own.

Socioeconomic status, foreign language programs that offer multiple languages, and offering courses off-campus that truly pique students' interests and training needs, such as culinary, woodshop, or mechanics, are other ways to demonstrate diversity. From credit recovery to accelerated courses, students are taken into consideration and the school works to address these diverse needs.

POLITICS

By politics, it is not the political parties that we are addressing, but the overall silent workings within a school system. The politics within a school or district can be wicked to work with, but often inevitable.

It is through politics that many times people obtain positions or are overlooked for promotion. It is through politics that some programs are funded while others are not. It is through politics that recipients of awards or scholarships are decided. Placements are often political, as are replacements. In many places, the "good ol' boy" network is still alive and well, while the situation is screaming for reformation of the system. Who are the decision makers in your district? How long have they been in power? Do they have the best interests of the students at heart, or are their decisions politically charged? How do you change the situation without getting yourself ousted in the process?

ACTIVITIES

What's most important to your school? Is it service leadership where your students are heavily involved in community and volunteer work? In situations such as this, students participate in programs that support perhaps local elderly homes, homeless shelters, or food banks. Student Council may be instrumental in organizing some of these events.

Athletics is an important program because of the exposure it brings to both schools and players. Local papers cover events, adding pictures of superstars. Reputations of players are built, and those who are sought after for scholarships add pride to the district. Pep rallies, dances, and Booster Club activities unite the school, both parents and students. Ongoing rivalries or defending of titles adds to the excitement and the pride of belonging to a particular group.

Other activities may not stir the public as an athletic program does, but are just as important to offer since students' needs and interests vary. A theatrical performance may not fill all of the seats, but the skills students learn as they work their way through a performance may inspire a student to seek an area as a career. Students who participate in forensics practice speaking in front of an audience, which helps develop skills and confidence for later years.

It is through communication that the general public can grow to understand skills developed through activities. Utilizing a local newspaper, inviting the public in for assemblies and programs, and celebrating accomplishments are all ways to connect the school with the community.

One of the most important lessons a new administrator can put into motion is not to change things right away. Doing this causes people to think that the incoming administrator thought they were doing things incorrectly or ineffectively. By taking the time to observe, question how and why, get the inside scoop on traditions, and connect with people, you build respect and trust.

SCHOOL CULTURE—ACTIVITY

Develop a way to obtain information to help you understand the culture of the school. This may be creation of an advisory committee made up of a few staff, parents, and students. Perhaps an early morning listening session where coffee and donuts are served to different target groups: board members one month, parents of K–2 another, grandparents another, parents of students in activities, and so on. Share your plan.

Develop a list of questions you would like to investigate during your first year. What are you curious about? What do you feel you need to know? What have you heard about that you want to know the history of or know more about? Now align those questions with the groups you wish to connect with so you can ask those questions of those groups. You may wish to ask the same questions of multiple groups to compare the answers and gain better insight.

SCHOOL CULTURE—REFLECTION

Think back to your school days. Break it up by level: elementary, middle, and secondary years. What do you remember from each as being significant to you in your development or piquing your interest in new areas? Were there special assignments you couldn't wait to get from specific teachers? Did the band program start in a certain grade?

Elementary

Middle

Secondary

With budget cuts at the forefront of many minds, how will you find out what's important to your school and your community, and what commitment are you willing to make to ensure students have opportunities to participate in activities?

8

Planning

STRATEGIC PLANNING

Strategic planning may be time consuming, but proves to be well worth the effort if the plan is referred to regularly and there is follow-through. Through strategic planning, boards, parents, and school personnel are brought together to clarify the vision of the community with regard to the role of the school. Strategic planning takes the pulse of the community's commitment and creates a plan that focuses the budget by determining which programs are important.

Through the lens of a community, limitations and access of resources are viewed, and there is determination of use of these precious resources. All aspects of the district/school are considered: facilities, school safety, curriculum, instruction, assessment, text/media adoption, technology, personnel (including mentoring/orientation, training, professional development, and continued education), and so forth. From the general, specific areas are targeted and an action plan is created.

Strategic planning assists in identifying who you are, what needs to be done, what resources you have and need, problems and critical issues, focus and priorities. With these areas identified, objectives can be identified and an action plan can be implemented including participants and timelines.

Strategic planning is an ongoing process that lends itself to school improvement. While the length of the cycle may vary, strategic planning has long-term (over four years) and short-term (one to three years) goals. The plan is meant to change, meaning that as items within the plan are completed, they should be noted and you move on, creating new goals within the process of replenishment. If working on a long-term goal, don't be afraid to rephrase goals or scrap ideas.

Once the strategic plan is created and board approved, you have your blueprint of the direction of the school both short and long term for the life of the plan. This helps greatly with decision making in that all decisions should align with the plan.

This means that if a parent comes to you and wants a new program, initially you can assess the alignment of the request with the plan and make a determination as to whether to proceed or not. For example, a parent requests intramurals after school. It is a goal listed within your strategic plan that you (the school) will provide extracurricular activities for the students. This aligns with your plan and you then proceed with looking into student interest, gym availability, supervision, transportation, and so on.

Another beauty of the plan is that you have good reason not to proceed on every request of every parent, board, or community member. If the request is not directly aligned to the plan, then this is not an area of focus for the school at this time. Keeping in alignment with the plan, you can state that you would be happy to reconsider this request as a committee when the life of this plan comes to term and a new one is developed.

NEEDS ASSESSMENTS

A needs assessment is the process of collecting information in order to improve current performance or correct a deficiency. Deficiencies are not necessarily a deficit in comparison to expectations or standards, but rather a gap between best practices and the school's current practice that proves problematic.

Needs assessments can be formal or informal and use different types of analysis. Ultimately, we want to answer the familiar questions of who, what, when, why, and how. Answering these questions will determine who will be involved (target population analysis); what the best way to perform would be (task analysis); when the process should take place with regard to breaks, budget, and so on (contextual analysis); why provide resources toward the need and what benefits you expect to see with the application of these resources (feasibility analysis and needs vs. wants analysis); and how the deficiency will be rectified (performance analysis).

In addition to identifying appropriate solutions, a needs assessment also assures that resources are set aside, meaning they are conserved and may only be used for the identified purpose. The process involves gathering existing information or developing new, analyzing it in a collaborative setting that includes all stakeholders, and creating a plan of how you will resolve the deficiencies. Delving deeper into the process, the needs assessment can serve as the basis from which SMART goals or a strategic plan are formed.

Since needs assessments can be formal or informal, school leadership must determine who will be involved, to what extent, and how information will be gathered. Data can be gathered in a number of ways, depending on what you are looking to analyze, with five techniques to collect the data: existing, attitude survey, key informant, community, and focus group.

Existing data analyzes what your school is already collecting: demographics, free/reduced lunch numbers, test scores, referrals, and such. Attitude survey collects information through interviews, surveys, and questionnaires. Key informant identifies those leaders and decision makers who are knowledgeable and have the capability to identify and prioritize concerns. Community forums are open to the public and allow all to express their concerns. This also offers insight into perceptions within the community. Utilizing a focus group would identify people for specific skills, expertise, views, or positions and be used as a cross-section or representation of the community. The focus group may have teachers, parents, students, administrators, and community members as members, each sharing his or her own viewpoints, experience, and expertise on a given topic.

Which of the techniques in the prior paragraph does the following reflect? Budget cuts are calling for some changes in your offering of electives. You don't want to make the decision alone on where these cuts will take place. You create a survey to share with different groups (teachers, students, parents, board, community) explaining there may need to be budget cuts and you want to see what's on people's minds. Subject areas required by state mandate for graduation are not on the list for consideration. Your list includes art courses, band, choir, drama/theatre, foreign language, photography, astronomy, and elective physical education courses. You have staff, students, and parents rank the electives in the order they see as important. This information leaves you with conclusive feedback, which would then be taken into consideration during planning and budget meetings where action must then be determined. This is an example of the attitude survey.

SMART GOALS

SMART goals are commonly used in the field of education; however, they were first used in November 1981's issue of *Management Review* in an article by George Doran, Arthur Miller, and James Cunningham. SMART is a mnemonic for Specific, Measurable, Attainable, Relevant, and Timely. Many times SMART goals are spin-offs of the strategic plan, as it sometimes seems more manageable to view the goals of the school in smaller chunks than to digest a large document. Let's look at each part.

Specific: Each goal is to be clearly stated. Identify who, what, where, when, which, and why. This refers to who is involved, what needs to be accomplished, the logistics or physical structures involved, time frame of completion or multiple time frames with listed accomplishments for each segment, resources needed to accomplish the goal, potential obstacles, and benefits of completion.

Measurable: Determine how you will measure success and progress of the goal. Determine the importance of meeting deadlines within the time line. Identify interventions you will put in place should you not reach targets, whether they be dates or data.

Attainable: Consider the attitudes, abilities, skills, finances, obstacles, and resources needed to accomplish this goal.

Relevant: Ask if the goal is feasible. Are participants willing and able to do what is needed to meet this goal? As you work on goals, do not be afraid to restructure, reword, or reconsider goals. Remain flexible and open to adjustments. Keep in mind that when you begin a remodeling project, you often come across other projects that you didn't intend on doing, but they now must be done as a foundation or in support of the original project. The same is with school goals. Challenges may redirect or deflect the original goal altogether. Baby steps may not have been the plan, but they still demonstrate progress toward the end goal.

Timely: Goals must have a time frame. The idea is that you work toward the goal, complete it, and replace it with a new, more pertinent goal. A time line also assists with maintaining focus for participants. If people are not held to some type of schedule to complete or report on their portion of the goal, those points may fall by the wayside and never reach completion.

Since its inception in 1981, SMART goals have often become SMARTER goals, adding Evaluate and Reward. Under Evaluate, goals are reviewed when accomplished. Participants look at what went well, what didn't, if the anticipated benefits have been enjoyed, challenges along the way, and the process under which the goal was met. The Reward component encourages participants to celebrate the completion of the goal as a motivator and way to encourage meeting future goals.

BUDGETS

Your participation in the development, defense, execution, and tracking of the school budget will depend on the structure within your district. Autonomy often allows building principals the responsibility of a building budget. Under this structure, line items may call for you to make decisions, such as personnel assignments/cuts and technology, right down to general purchases for art supplies and paper.

Superintendents, district administrators, and other district-level administrators may find themselves charged with responsibility of the overall budget and making decisions for large purchases such as text adoptions, copy machines, or technology. Then smaller amounts are funneled to the school to meet everyday needs. Often the allocations are based on enrollment.

The budget process will depend on the resources utilized by the district or school, depending on your placement. Public schools are often connected to specific software due to state requirements. Nonpublic schools may develop budgets based on the requirements of their financial supporter, whether it is software utilized, a charter, tuition, vouchers, grants—take all into consideration.

Don't be afraid to ask for assistance. Utilize your mentor, but also inquire about other resources available. Every state has a department of education (though they may go by different titles), and often these offices will offer special workshops for new administrators, particularly to learn software, understand available funding, and model accurate completion of required reports.

GROWTH

There are many ways a district can demonstrate growth. We often equate the success of the district or administration with student achievement; however, education is multifaceted.

Investing in faculty through targeted professional development, continued education, and professional learning communities can demonstrate growth from investment in quality teachers from which our students then benefit. Defining long- and short-term goals within the district can assist with the focus of finances and resources. Successful completion of these goals can demonstrate growth. Revision of curriculum, instruction, or programs based on review of data and ongoing evaluation can also demonstrate growth.

It is important that we remain open-minded, particularly since we are often spokespeople to the parents and larger community, to help others understand both the challenges and the successes educators address within the system.

PLANNING—ACTIVITY

As you learn more about planning, consider the following with regard to your district's planning process.

The board is proactive and not reactive in nature.
The board focuses on (a) policy, (b) personnel, (c) curriculum/instruction, (d) student achievement, (e) other.
The board regularly allows public speaking, listens to participants, and openly considers input in its decision-making process.
The board understands and utilizes data in decision making.
The board understands that change takes time.
The board works together well for the good of the students in the district.
Conflict is handled in a straightforward and assertive manner.
Board meetings are held regularly, are well organized and productive, and follow format.
There is a good relationship between district administration and the board.
There is good communication between district administration and the board.
There is joint decision making between district administration and the board.
There is a good understanding on behalf of the board regarding best practices and the resources needed to attain such.
There is good community response to the needs of the district.
The community is financially supportive of the district.
There is collaboration between the district, community, and board for both long-term and short-term planning.

Chapter 8

PLANNING—REFLECTION

What do I know about the planning process of my current district? What is my role? What is my comfort zone? Which areas do I feel most comfortable with, and in which areas do I feel I may need some assistance?

Based on preliminary interactions in my district and particularly within my building, three goals that I would like to initially identify for consideration for review and possible action are:

(1)

(2)

(3)

List below some people, their skill set, and possible roles for leadership or participation in strategic planning, needs assessments, and/or setting SMART goals in the future:

9

Starting the School Year: Between the Last Day and Staff Preparation Days

For students, summer lasts forever. June and July stretch on for eternity. Students do not think about school until late August when Mom takes them shopping for new shoes, clothing, and school supplies. Kids do not plan for the first day of school. They just show up.

Stating the obvious, summer for school principals lasts only a very few short days, during which they must complete planning for the coming year. Not that it's in progress. Not sort of done, as in "we can use temporary rooms until the painters finish"; not sort of done, as in "we can fix up the schedule when we see how many students have mistakes"; not sort of done as in "well, we still have some staff vacancies; we'll use subs."

Principals must be guided by a minor change of the old political statement— "As the first day of school goes, so goes the school year." Maybe. If everything is ready to go and the first day of school is flawless, that gets the year off to a good start, and the school year has strong possibilities of being a good one. If, however, shoddy planning has caused a disastrous first day, that day predicts a poor school year, as the principal and staff spend an inordinate amount of teaching and learning time cleaning up the mess. Let's make it a good one.

THE FACILITY

The principal, working with the buildings and grounds department, if such exists in the school district, must assure that the school itself is ready for the first day.

Cleaning must be finished. Building cleaning requires a rigid time schedule, perhaps a complex schedule if the district assigns summer school or some other program like summer band to the facility. Whatever the constraints, the custodians must have completed their work. If necessary, the principal should get authorization for weekend or late hour overtime work and pay.

The cleaning schedule, planned in advance prior to the end of the school year, must be implemented and followed. While the lead engineer has the primary responsibility of supervising and managing the cleaning, the principal must monitor timelines and communicate to assure that the crew meets deadlines.

Maintenance projects must be complete, however complex or minuscule. If broken student desks are on the maintenance schedule, repair must be finished prior to the first day of school. Little things like pencil sharpeners to big things like replacing broken windows—all such projects must be completed. The principal and the maintenance supervisor must perform the same tasks as they did for cleaning: design a plan, implement it, supervise and manage it, and communicate frequently.

Frequently schools experience modernization or renovation during the summer. For example, a district may schedule a project requiring the replacement of old windows with ones that are more durable and more energy efficient. Or a district may schedule room modifications involving replacement of old room lighting with improved and more energy efficient lighting. Or flooring containing asbestos may be replaced.

Completion of such projects often coincides with the cleaning schedule, thus complicating both projects. Nevertheless, the clock ticks. The renovation projects must move on schedule, the same as above: design a plan, implement it, supervise and manage it, and communicate frequently.

Careful advance planning, efficient work, and commitment to the timeline assure that the school itself is ready for students on the first day. The custodial staff, the buildings and grounds staff, and outside contractors have the responsibility to supervise all of the above referenced activities. However, the principal must involve him- or herself in the process, meeting frequently through the summer with the project supervisors. If the school is ready, the building itself leads to the prediction of a successful school year.

Share the plan with your staff. Let your teachers know when they can get into the building to set up and get their classrooms ready even if it means one wing or floor is ready for occupancy before another. Some teachers like to get in early, even if the contract has not officially started. When you send out your call-back letter, be sure to share dates and times the building will be open.

STAFF

Although the HR (department or person) takes care of staffing issues, the school principal must commit to the process throughout the summer. A short staff predicts a poor start to the school year. Starting the year with unfilled positions, substitutes in positions, or vacancies in positions due to late increased enrollment causes chaos on the first day of school.

Therefore:

- All teaching sections must be filled.
- All administrative positions must be filled.
- All custodial positions must be filled.
- All educational assistant positions must be filled.
- All support staff (counselor, social worker, and psychologist) positions must be filled.

Period.

Other people in the district have the responsibility of staffing. However, a fully staffed school, on the first day of school, is the responsibility of the principal. Advance planning and effective communication throughout the process, especially for changes late in the summer, are essential.

STUDENT SERVICES

Preparing the master schedule is a subject for an entire book. However, for this work, to sum up the process, by the first bell on the first day of the school year, the master schedule must be complete. Shuffling around, moving sections, or changing student schedules all make for a poor beginning and predict a poor school year. All known students must be registered, each having a full and accurate schedule. The principal must have a plan ready for registering and scheduling new walk-in students. All special needs students must have schedules as determined by the IEP. For a great start to the school year, all of these are absolutes.

TEACHER SERVICES

This section more or less goes back to the basics. However, new administrators must pay careful attention to the importance of one's relationship with teachers; furthermore, experienced administrators may need a brush up. No principal wants to begin a school year with frustrated and angry teachers. Preplanning and careful implementation resolve the issue of teacher frustration and anger, replacing it with anticipation of a successful school year.

A new administrator should send staff an introduction letter: Who Am I? Where Do I Come From? Where Have I Worked? What Are My Expectations? These are just examples. Suffice it to say that teachers want to know about their new administrator before they walk in the door.

Teachers expect a "Welcome Back" letter. This letter could contain a number of things: present enrollment, progress on building preparations, what's new? A welcome back letter consisting of specific information, rather than general platitudes, helps set a positive teacher/principal climate.

Teachers want to know their teaching assignments. The principal should consider mailing home a copy of each teacher's schedule. Learning the assignment on the first workday for the teacher causes frustration. The teacher schedule may be mailed home with the welcome back letter. However, a personal letter accompanied by a copy of the schedule has a more positive effect.

PREPARATION OF STUDENT/PARENT COMMUNICATION

Students and parents need to know many things in order to prepare for the first day of school. Most of this information usually appears in the summer newsletter, discussed below. Hence, just a short list works here:

What are the start and dismissal times?
Where is my bus pickup location?
What are the requirements for physical education uniforms?
Is there a dress code that students and/or teachers need to follow?
Do I need to file a free/reduced lunch application?
What is the plan for the first school day?
What are the rules of behavior for the school?

These are just examples. Over the course of the summer, the principal should review, from his notes and his experiences, all the questions that parents and students ask. The questions all need answers prior to the first day of school.

When a layperson asks school principals what they do in the summer, it confirms that she or he does not know the scope of the position.

LEADERSHIP AND MENTORING

Leadership Activities

- Liaise with district personnel to remain current with changes in policy and/or procedure.

- Prepare an event calendar that identifies deadlines for each summer event, especially the scheduling process.
- Delegate responsibilities appropriately.
- Complete personal responsibilities according to the established calendar.
- Supervise and assist with the completion of delegated responsibilities.
- Anticipate challenges and prepare for resolving them.

Mentorship Activities

- Review all start-up preparations for the next school year with all experienced staff.
- Mentor new staff step by step in all aspects of start-up preparations.
- Carefully supervise all staff involved in start-up preparations. Commend, assist, and correct as necessary.
- Carefully review all completed tasks. Commend or direct correction as necessary.

CONCLUSIONS AND REFLECTIONS

An effective leader/mentor behaves proactively. Planning for a coming school year cannot be based on correcting mistakes. The major responsibilities for a school principal, aside from completing activities that are the province of the directing principal, are: leading, motivating, monitoring, and assisting.

An effective leader anticipates very long days over the course of the summer. This may include many late nights. An effective leader takes minimal, carefully scheduled vacation days. An effective leader understands that effective and timely completion of activities outlined in the "Starting the School Year" segments predicts an excellent start of the school year and prevents a chaotic start.

THE FIRST DAY

Starting the school year actually begins the preceding spring with planning, scheduling, and drafting documents for situations that lead up to the first bell on opening day. Though time lines vary by district, the tasks are similar. Careful preparation and anticipation of challenges create a successful opening day. While opening day procedures vary from school district to school district and from school to school, most plans should answer the following questions.

Where do students report? This is something that the summer newsletter addresses. In a small elementary school, for instance, the summer newsletter tells students to report to a specific room or a specific teacher's room. If the school has more than one teacher per grade level, summer communication must identify the room assignment for each student. Many districts have an orientation day in the week preceding the first day of school. Locating homerooms, meeting teachers, receiving instructions about needed supplies, and so on facilitate the first day.

Clear instructions for initial reporting can assist in alleviating first-day jitters on all levels: students, staff, and parents. At the elementary level, students may be asked to report to the auditorium or the gym for an opening assembly, or perhaps a specific door on the playground based on teacher assignment.

For middle and high school students, mailing the students' schedules home within two weeks prior to the first day is a good solution. This choice gives students a chance to review their schedules for accuracy, and it gives them the chance to contact the school so that the scheduler can make the necessary changes. Missing classes, classes double scheduled, and no lunch period scheduled are some of the things that can be corrected if the students get their schedules in the days prior to the start of school.

Schools frequently offer a schedule pick-up day, designating a specific day for each grade level. This activity gives parents an opportunity to pay fees, such as book rental or athletic fees, or purchase yearbooks in advance.

Despite a good plan for getting schedules to students, there are some who do not, for whatever reason, receive the schedules. The principal must anticipate this. The principal must designate schedule pick-up rooms—by grade level, by alphabet, or by whatever means that fits the school—to which students report. Plans must include staffing the rooms. Careful planning gets students to the right place at the right time, allowing a smooth start for the first day.

What is the theme of the first all-school announcement? A motivational statement, a quick review of behavior expectations, encouragement to ask questions throughout the day—these serve as perhaps obvious topics for the first announcement.

Most importantly, the first announcement should set the tone or the climate of the school. Summer's over. It's time to get on task, treat everyone with respect, and behave appropriately. And it's time for the principal to be brief. A lengthy all-school announcement at the beginning of the first day loses effectiveness after the first minute. Careful planning makes the first announcement effective.

What is the process for registering and scheduling new students? Lack of a plan causes disruption and confusion. Poorly thought-out plans cause problems down the road. An example of a poorly thought-out plan: Give a new student the schedule of a student who did not show up on the first day. The transfer from paper to computer can occur later. Think about thirty students running through the school with someone else's schedule, but not appearing on any teacher's class list.

Have a plan for how you will deal with a situation such as this. This will make life easier for you, the students, and the teachers. Most new students report first to the school office. It makes sense to send those students to another place for getting their schedules. In a middle school, for instance, a student could report to the grade-level counselor. The counselor then designs a schedule and passes it over to the scheduling assistant principal who enters it into the computer. After a short wait, the student goes off to class with a legitimate schedule.

Of course, new students make changes to teachers' class lists. So the scheduling principal must plan the printing and distribution of new class lists as quickly as possible. This whole process may continue for several days. The key of a good plan is getting new students registered, scheduled, and off to class as quickly and efficiently as possible with communication to the teachers.

What is the role of the principal on the first day? This choice is up to the principal, but he or she must think about this ahead of time. Visit each classroom? Assist with registering and scheduling students? Monitor class sizes? Participate in each lunch period? Be visible: parking lot, bus duty, and hallways? Explain the dismissal process in an all-school announcement at the end of the school day? Help students find their way around the school? The options are many. The principal must expect and plan for activities far different from those on a typical school day.

The tone of the first day of school sets the tone for the whole school year. A chaotic first day predicts a chaotic year. A day in which students get settled and oriented predicts a good year. A day in which teaching and learning begin predicts a great year.

STARTING UP THE SCHOOL YEAR—ACTIVITY

Thinking of all of the "things" you need to do as the new school year approaches can be overwhelming. Make a list. Prioritize it. Determine your resources (i.e., who can assist you in each area). Delegate. Monitor. Stay on top of the situation.

Facility:

Preparation of Staff:

Preparation of Student Services:

Preparation of Teacher Services:

Preparation of Communication:

STARTING UP THE SCHOOL YEAR—REFLECTION

Whether the start of the school year is approaching or you have been hired mid-year and are preparing to take on the duties of your new position, reflect on the following:

What am I most anxious about? Why is it causing anxiety, and what can I do to create a situation where I do not feel anxious?

Am I prepared?

Am I organized?

Do I have a support system in place?

Have I communicated clearly, and to all of the stakeholders as necessary?

Do I know the expectations of my position?

Do I understand whom I report to, ask questions of, and obtain support in my new position?

What role do I want my mentor to take during these hectic first days?

How can my mentor assist me?

Do my mentor and I have time scheduled both prior to and after the first day activities?

10

School Safety and Crisis Management

THE BASICS OF SCHOOL SAFETY AND CRISIS MANAGEMENT

Let's begin with a few definitions:

School Safety: Policies and behaviors that keep students free from harm and that allow effective performance in situations where the potential of harm exists.
Crisis: An event or series of events that potentially or actually cause harm to the school population, including students and all staff.
Crisis Management: Policies and behaviors that prevent, minimize, and resolve crisis situations.

For purposes of discussion, assume that schools have safety procedures in place for labs, physical education, technical education, home economics, and art classes. Such policies are in place almost universally.

In best practice cases, the teacher, department, or department supervisor writes the safety practices. Teachers give copies of the safety procedures to all students. Students share the safety procedures. Parents read and sign off on the procedures. Students return the signed safety document to the teacher, who keeps them on file to document that students and parents know the procedures. As a given responsibility, teachers supervise students effectively, to assure that they are using the safety procedures.

This chapter concerns crisis management, not the same plans explored in the above paragraph. Readers should view the following statements as absolutes, in that all school districts must comply with the following principles.

Every school district must have a district safety and crisis management plan. This plan has two purposes. First, the plan covers policies and practices that deal with a crisis that impacts the whole school district. Second, the plan serves as an umbrella for crisis management plans for each school. The district plan is a guide for the school plans.

All personnel in central administration must know all components of the plan and must have the authority and ability to implement the plan. This represents the "need to know" concept. To know all the components of the plan means that central administration personnel must have mastered the plan, as much as possible. The district plan must have a chain of command structure, allowing subordinates to initiate the plan if the safety director, assistant superintendent, or superintendent is not able to do so.

Every school must have a safety and crisis management plan. As stated above, the school plan may share components with the district plan; however, each school has its own characteristics. Where do students report for a fire drill? Where do students report for a tornado drill? Is your school a hurricane shelter? What is the emergency off-site location? Are local TV/radio stations used to get the word out for early closures due to inclement weather? Do the parents know to which station the school or district reports?

The school principal and all staff at every given school must have full knowledge of and the ability to initiate all components of the school crisis plan. Note that this statement does not mean that any staff member may initiate the crisis plan. As stated above, the school plan must have a chain of command structure. Also, school administrators need general knowledge of the district crisis plan.

Communication tools and procedures must be in place. These tools and procedures facilitate the necessary communication between all administrators and other key personnel in any given school, all district administrators responsible for crisis response, all police agencies that may respond to a crisis, all fire and rescue agencies that may respond to a crisis, and all emergency management agencies. This presents a very complex, and expensive, communication process. The Leadership and Mentoring for Safety and Crisis Management sections, which appear below, address the components of the communication structure.

Districts must mandate regular practices and review of the following crisis response actions: school entrance doors lockdown, secure in place lockdown, short-term evacuation for fire and other potential situations, tornado and other move to in-school safety locations, and long-term evacuations to a predetermined alternate site. These actions define the basic responses to a crisis. Regular practice and review of these procedures reduce panic and mixed, garbled commands issued on the spur of the moment. Practice also gives students and staff experience with the procedures. Practices greatly reduce the breakdown of the crisis response.

Development, practice, and review predict successful implementation of any and all aspects of crisis plans. "It won't happen here" does not constitute a reason for not practicing the complicated activities outlined above. Districts must plan.

LEADERSHIP FOR SAFETY AND CRISIS MANAGEMENT

Leadership regarding safety and crisis management refers to design and practice. Rather than starting from scratch, crisis managers may use templates available online as a guide for designing district-specific and school-specific plans. Googling "school safety plans" leads to a number of options.

The school district must design and implement safety and crisis management plans if none are present. The district plan must state all responses for crises that have the potential of involving the whole district. The district plan must also serve as an umbrella for school plans. The district administrator/director of school safety should/must liaise with school principals to assist in designing and implementing plans for all schools in the district.

The school district, in cooperation with emergency services, must design a communication system that provides the ability for schools, the district safety coordinator and other central administrators, and emergency services to communicate effectively with each other.

This aspect of crisis plan design utilizes two basic tools—cell phones and radios. Design of cell phone use in a crisis situation is relatively easy: district personnel load into their address books all pertinent telephone numbers. These include the phone numbers of all district administrators responsible for crisis management, especially the person designated as safety director. Other pertinent numbers include those for police, fire, and emergency management agencies.

Cell phones obviously meet the need for one-on-one communication between individuals. This works for summoning agency response, for notification of the district safety director or other appropriate central administration personnel, and for communication between specific school personnel.

The second tool requires careful design and likely the expenditure of a lot of money: the use of radio communication. Ideally, radio communication allows contact between central administration and all school principals: school principals, assistant principals, and administrators between various schools. Basically design of effective radio communication requires good five-watt portable radios (walkie-talkies) with common frequencies and the ability to switch between multiple frequencies.

Effective communication may also require the appropriate placement and use of repeaters, which are powerful transmitter/receivers that rebroadcast transmissions from the five-watt radios. Putting it simply, in this work, school districts should employ communication consultants who work to assist in designing the appropriate system for the specific district. Suffice it to say that radio communication is essential in crisis management.

Two activities complete the leadership of school safety and crisis management. Districts must mandate regular practices for fire drills and tornado or hurricane warnings. For fire drills monthly is a good idea. That means monthly. It does not mean skipping the cold weather months and catching up in spring. For tornado or hurricane drills, practice before and during the season is adequate. Serious crisis situations need practice at least annually. These include school entrance lockdowns, secure in place lockdowns, and long-term evacuation to the predetermined alternate site.

Effective design and practice of school safety and crisis management procedures are good predictors of effective implementations.

MENTORING FOR SAFETY AND CRISIS MANAGEMENT

Depending on the size of your district, this area could look very different. For larger districts with a central office of administrators, the chain of command moves along from the individual school, to central office, perhaps to a crisis management director and/or the superintendent for implementation and decision making along the way. Other schools may be part of a feeder district so there may be only one school within the district, or a school may be independent (parochial, Charter, choice, etc.), and in these schools, it is typically the principal on whom all planning, implementing, and decision making falls.

Using the example of a larger district, one would be using experts in the field to help design a district plan, and mentoring begins with administrators at central office. This mentorship first shows, then teaches that administrator how to design a plan specific for the district. The expert does not merely pull a plan out of the laptop and show the administrator how to use it. Mentoring continues through the plan design process.

The next step in mentoring school safety and crisis management involves the central administrator and the district school administrators. Mentorship at this level concerns teaching school principals all details of the overall district plan. The district safety and crisis administrator could use a meeting of all school principals to teach the district plan. Then mentorship steps to the design of plans for the individual schools. In this phase of the process, the district safety and crisis person works specifically with a school's principal and assistant principals for the design of the plan.

In the third step in mentoring, the administrator for safety and crisis managing mentors the district-wide plan to all central administrators. This mentorship includes the directors of any contracted service such as transportation.

In the fourth step of the mentoring process, the school administrator responsible for safety and crisis management mentors all workers in the school, including teachers, educational assistants, security personnel, the head engineer, all custodians, and all cafeteria employees. The administrator provides copies of the plan to each employee. The administrator then goes over all aspects of the plan. This mentorship would use two or three all-staff meetings dedicated only to the plan.

Teachers, with the help of the school administrator for safety and crisis, mentor students. This mentorship works best one teacher, one class at a time. Obviously, the process requires quite a bit of time and a very specific schedule to which teachers and administrators must adhere. In this process, each student gets a written copy of the school plan.

Finally, in an evening parent meeting, to which all parents have received a written invitation, the school safety administrator mentors parents. Like the students, parents get copies of the plan. Why distribute documents to both parents and students? Parents and students need the written copy for reference should the need for implementation become necessary. For example, in a long-term off-site evacuation, parents must know the process by which they report to the site and check out their children.

Applying this to smaller districts or independent schools, the steps remain the same though the players will be different. Smaller districts often combine as consortiums to share resources and share information. This group may choose to work together, much as a central office, to design a model plan reflective of the needs of their area, and then draft a plan specific to one's school with that master plan in place.

Independent schools often have a connection, such as parochial schools being part of a larger archdiocese, a charter school under the sponsorship of a local business or university, or a choice school being connected to a community church. Administrators serving these schools need to make sure they understand the chain of command on-site and off, meaning often the principal is on-site and solely charged with all areas of running the school, including safety.

However, there may be resources available through the larger umbrella through which a master plan is offered, with the school creating a plan that would be implemented locally. As with larger districts, the important piece is that all stakeholders know the plan and time has been dedicated for discussion and practice.

This whole mentorship process is very time consuming and very intensive. The end result, however, justifies the time and effort: Everyone knows the plan.

WHAT PROBABLY NEEDS CHANGING RIGHT AWAY

The drafting, or even a review of an existing crisis management plan, should include a study of what works, what is complete as it is, and what should change as soon as possible.

Communication systems frequently need improvement. For example, when individual schools decide to implement radio communication, the responsible person shops for two-way radios, buys what he or she thinks is a good product (likely including preprogrammed frequencies), brings the product back to the school, and begins using it. One school might have something entirely different from another school. Radios range from the old CB two-ways, to the small devices used to communicate between hunters, to variations on low-end professional two-way radios.

From school to school, the operating transmission/reception frequencies may differ completely. If this is the case, the school district must plan an efficient communication plan, with all schools using a given brand of radio, with all schools transmitting on the same frequency (in best practice, using radios with multiple channels, so one frequency is reserved for elementary schools, one is used for middle schools, one is used for high schools, and one is used for all district communication).

This is another time-consuming process, involving study of what is in place, designing an all-district communication system, purchase of the product, installation of school master antennas, and mentoring. It is also very expensive, though the school district has a responsibility to provide funds and specifications for the above.

Practice of the lockdown procedures and the all-school extended off-site evacuation likely does not exist. The rationale is that such practice would scare students, is very complicated, and takes too much time.

The question is: what would happen if these procedures must be implemented? Fear would be there anyway, despite practice. And panic would be there because students and teachers would not know what to do. For example, in a real situation, during passing time, a principal gets on the public address system and announces, "We are implementing a secure in place lockdown. All students immediately report to the closest classroom. Teachers, lock up when the halls are clear." What would happen?

Planning and practice take a lot of time, a lot of in-service, and a lot of money. But all are necessary. Leadership and mentorship intertwine in the review and redesign processes.

LEADERSHIP AND MENTORING FOR PERIODIC REVIEW

Districts must perform periodic review of safety and crisis plans to ensure that they all are up to date. The leader schedules the interview and leads the review meetings. Reviews may include the following points:

Review what aspects of the plan are currently in place.
Review of the drill and practice record.
Review plans which require design, practice, and implementation.
Review must cover both the district plan and the plans of individual schools. Written records document the review and help calendar the deadline for plan modifications.

Continuing mentorship of safety and crisis plans is obviously necessary. New personnel, such as a new assistant principal, need to know all aspects of the school plan as well as general knowledge of the district plan. All staff members need periodic review. Staff meetings seem to be the best venues for such a review. Safety and crisis plans that gather dust on bookshelves or are buried deep in desk drawers are useless.

Some concluding thoughts are appropriate at this juncture. Let's assume the obvious: Safety of students is top priority. Never take for granted that existing plans will "always work." Always anticipate the unexpected and have a plan that allows "making it up as you go along" within the parameters of the overall plan. Always define and use effective mentorship. Practice counts as mentorship. Never cause people to run around shouting, "What should I do now?" This is very serious business.

SCHOOL SAFETY AND
CRISIS MANAGEMENT—ACTIVITY

What do you know about your school's safety plan and your role? Review both the district and school safety plans, noting the role you would have in each.

Is the plan current? If not, what is the process for change of such a document within your school/district?

Do others know the plan and know their roles? Have conversations with other administrators at both the district and school levels. Ensure that each is aware of and practices the plan in place.

How is the plan communicated with staff? Students? Parents? Is there direction to the parents on where to go or not go, how to communicate (text or phone), or policies and/or directions on picking up your children during a crisis? Are staff and support staff aware of these instructions?

SCHOOL SAFETY AND CRISIS MANAGEMENT—REFLECTION

Of what are you most afraid?

How could this play into your leadership role during a crisis?

What could you do to personally remain calm, cool, and collected—effective—during a crisis?

Have you been in a crisis situation before? If so, how did you handle it? What did you do well, and what do you think you could have done better or would do differently if that situation arose again?

During a crisis, what characteristics do you think are most important to the staff and students entrusted to your care, and how can you follow through on those?

11

Time Management

ORGANIZATION

We all have our own style of organization. Some people have everything lined up on their desks and use manila folders, binders, and a color-coded filing system. Other people have papers strewn across a desk, sometimes spilling on to piles on the floor, yet when asked, they can produce the necessary documents. It is important that we know what works for us.

Organization affects areas such as recordkeeping and planning. Administrative duties affected by one's organization include submitting receipts for an expense report, preparing paperwork for funding, gathering documents for an audit, and tracking budgetary allocations and spending. Planning of assemblies, parent events, and programs are directly affected by organization.

RUNNING AN EFFECTIVE MEETING

Time is a commodity, and no one wants to sit in a meeting that seems unproductive or unorganized. Take into consideration the frequency that the group meets, and set up an agenda that focuses on items that need to be addressed. As the facilitator, provide a time frame to attendees and keep the meeting on task. Should members get into a discussion beyond the target items, encourage them to get together after the meeting concludes, or to set up another time to focus on the item.

Have a defined time for the group to meet, and discuss expectations. For example, a mandatory meeting such as a monthly staff meeting needs to be taken seriously by staff so people don't make other plans or schedule appointments thinking they can just talk their way out of the meeting. Decide if and what the ramifications will be for staff who miss meetings. With committee meetings such as textbook adoption, curriculum development, Sunshine Committee, or school assemblies, the expectations must be shared. As a membership, decide on attendance (i.e., do members need to make every meeting, or will different departments or levels hold meetings alternately with the whole group?).

The agenda should follow a routine format, and be made available in advance to the group. Input from group members may be solicited prior to determining the agenda, or agenda items may be added as part of the approval of the agenda during the actual meeting. Be sure to provide the agenda prior to the meeting. You may wish to send a reminder to the group, including the date, time, and location of the meeting. If meeting via technology, be sure to give instruction as to log-in information or codes necessary. Be sure to give time for questions, comments, announcements, and brainstorming.

Meetings take place for different reasons: information, brainstorming, problem solving, decision making, reporting, or assigning workload. Depending on the purpose of the meeting, you may introduce the problem and give time for discussion and ask open-ended questions. Leave opportunity for each person to share ideas, ask questions, and voice his or her opinion. At the end of your meeting, recap action items and the person(s) responsible for each.

Have someone in the group take notes. For regular meetings, you may wish to rotate this task. The person running the meeting should not be the one to take notes. Distribute meeting notes in a timely manner, including actionable items, responsible parties, and time lines. If you fail to follow up on these items, the meeting is not only viewed as a waste of time, but you lose credibility and respect of your staff.

Ask for feedback from group members regarding the smoothness of the meeting, as well as content and time on task. If you have good rapport with your staff, and openly communicate, they will feel comfortable sharing their feelings about the effectiveness of your meetings, as well as ways to improve. Use this evaluative process to plan improvements for the next meeting.

TAKING CARE OF YOURSELF

There are some ways that you can take care of yourself. First, don't be afraid to ask for help. If possible, delegate some of your responsibilities. Second, have a discussion with your supervisor. Be open with the overload of responsibilities and ask for assistance with prioritizing. Last, learn to take care of yourself.

Delegating responsibility gives employees challenges and the chance to grow. When delegating, think about people who have the skill set or interest in that area where they could handle the responsibility with little direct contact. You will be there for support, but you do not want to share the responsibility and then micromanage the person. You chose him or her because you knew he or she could handle the task. It improves your relationship with your staff because you demonstrate trust in their abilities. In the meantime, it takes some of the pressure and load off of you.

Having a discussion with your supervisor will take some preparation prior to your meeting. Take the time to make a list of what needs to be done, time lines and time commitment of each, and the order you feel they need to be done. If you hope to delegate the responsibility, list the person(s) and why you have them in mind for this particular task. Armed with this information, you demonstrate the time and thought you have put into the preparation. With the legwork done, you can have a candid discussion with your supervisor on prioritizing the tasks and delegating some of the projects.

Take care of yourself and learn to manage your stress. Three critical areas of managing in a high-stress environment are self-awareness, self-renewal, and self-management. Self-awareness is looking at current practices, reflecting, and changing as necessary. Self-renewal is finding ways to rejuvenate. Self-management is the search for strategies to deal with the demands of life.

Some people find refuge in individual activities such as jogging or walking, while others find group activities such as bowling or volleyball meet their needs. Some people are social and like to quilt or work on scrapbooks, cars, or other projects while others find solace in a quiet walk.

Taking a ride to get off-campus, taking a lunch, or calling a colleague on the phone are all ways to regroup. Sometimes people like to use breathing or counting exercises to relax. Focusing on the relaxation technique instead of the stress will prove more effective, and provide higher quality, more productive work. Decide how much anxiety a problem is worth, and refuse to give it more. Insomnia is not an option.

Sometimes administrators get into the mindset that they cannot take time off. One sign of a good leader is that staff can perform in the administrator's absence, so take it as a compliment that your staff doesn't need you there all of the time.

The school or office will run without you. It may run a little differently, but the reality is that life in the office will go on if we take a vacation, and unfinished projects will remain on our desk until our return. To manage stress effectively, you must learn to take time off, or if they continually schedule in meetings and events, your calendar will quickly fill. In addition, you need to learn to say no. It is easy for administrators to feel guilty if they don't attend an event, take on projects to be agreeable, or participate for the good of the cause; however, no one can be good at everything 24/7 and something will need to give.

Sometimes it helps to make a list of challenges and benefits, or pros and cons, of your job. Consider wages, benefits, flexibility, philosophy, relationships, competency of colleagues, room for growth and advancement, schedule of raises as well as percents, time required outside of regular business hours, type of work, amount of work, deadlines, and such. For those items you don't particularly care for, determine what you can change and develop a plan to do so. The areas you cannot change, decide how you will handle.

In these technological times, e-mails and voicemails are accessible 24/7. Determine preset times you will respond. It is imperative that you allow yourself down times, meaning even though accessible, you turn the technology off for awhile.

Create a network of support. This may include the mentor, but may be a colleague, friend, or family member. Network with other professionals in similar roles.

Cultivate a mental attitude that will bring you peace and happiness by filling your mind with positive thoughts of peace, courage, health, and hope. Never try to get even with your enemies, expect ingratitude, try to profit from your losses, create happiness for others, and count your blessings not your troubles (Carnegie, 1937).

Find the humor in situations. If you can laugh at yourself, it will ease the pressure and you know you don't have to be perfect all of the time. Try to find the humor in daily events as laughing relieves tension. While people don't appreciate childish behavior, they tend to support child-like behavior: goof, dance, sing, or play with a vengeance.

POSITIVE OUTCOMES OF EFFECTIVE MENTORING PROGRAMS

Providing support to a new employee has multiple benefits. From the physical perspective, an employee who is supported will be less likely to take sick days, or be worried, stressed, or anxious about his performance. Stress can do amazing things to the body, from losing hair to creating ulcers.

Increased retention within a position creates continuity within a staff, and is cost-effective for a district. The cost incurred with the replacement of staff can be great, as it covers ads, time for screening and interviewing, training, mentoring, and ongoing professional development.

A supportive mentoring program can bring learning to a new level for the participant. It can alleviate chaos and provide job satisfaction.

CHARACTERISTICS OF PEAK PERFORMERS

As a peak performer, one is committed to his physical, emotional, and spiritual being as well as personal growth and development. All are learned skills, which verify that anyone can be a peak performer if she or he is willing to commit.

There are many descriptors when looking at peak performers: focused, confident, persistent, tenacious, goal oriented, creative, high quality, high energy, driven, determined, relaxed, willing to practice, and bored with tasks below their abilities. Beliefs shape attitudes, and peak performers will have few to no self-limiting beliefs. High performers recognize their potential and display confidence. Often peak performers will practice visualization, such as seeing oneself win at a sport or earn a promotion. For example, at age four, Julia Mancuso drew a picture of herself winning the gold medal at the Olympics—and she won the gold at Torino in 2006.

They are risk takers and believe they will succeed in what they set out to do, which is critical to optimizing performance. Characteristics of peak performers include challenging oneself, reading journals, or listening to motivational tapes to stay current in the field. Peak performers set goals, continually evaluate, and are open to feedback. They are comfortable with who they are and where they want to be. Peak performers continually increase performance across the board.

TIME MANAGEMENT—ACTIVITY

Review three weeks of your calendar. Make them nonconsecutive weeks and in different times of the year. How did you fill your time? Do you recall how you felt during those periods? Over the next three (consecutive) weeks, keep tabs on how you fill your time. Be sure to schedule in time for yourself, whether it is exercising or reading. Record how you feel at the end of this period.

Look ahead. What long-range (later but within the school year) and short-range (within the next two weeks) projects do you have coming up? How are you preparing for them? What can you do now to make the event run smoother and allow you to enjoy rather than stress out over the event?

TIME MANAGEMENT—REFLECTION

List some time-management strengths that you hold.

List some counterproductive time-use habits you display.

Design an action plan to change the counterproductive time-use habits while building on your strengths.

Prioritize tasks for the upcoming week, differentiating those that are important but not urgent.

What was your biggest challenge as an administrator this past week?

12

Decision Making

Decision making is a very important process. You need to display the confidence and competency expected of leaders. When one avoids making a decision, it worsens the situation because employees may view you as incompetent, demonstrating a lack of follow-through, or avoiding difficult issues. A quick decision may be viewed as emotional, thoughtless, or harsh.

Take time to clearly define the problem. Investigate, discuss, and question the issue, and from multiple perspectives if possible. In other words, bring your team into the decision-making process whenever possible. Joint decision making offers clarity in how the issues are viewed, voiced, bought in to, and supported. Consider tentative solutions and analyze possibilities. Allow your intuition to be part of the process.

Whether you take notes as you investigate, or brainstorm with others on your team, give yourself time to process both the problems and possible solutions or resolution. In some situations you will not have an answer, but provide support and input.

Decisions may not be able to be put into place immediately. You need to give the decision a chance to be implemented and time for the changes to become practice. Monitor the situation so modifications can be made. You may want to scrap a decision, but do so only after careful consideration and obtaining evidence that what's in place is clearly not working.

Take the total impact of the decision into consideration. Systemic change may take years to see the impact of the change. Changes in policies or procedures may take time to go through proper channels. Some changes may be direct and swiftly implemented.

While it's great to take responsibility for decisions that people like or feel are successful, we must also remain accountable for those decisions that may not be so popular or didn't turn out as well as we'd hoped. Leaders must be willing to make decisions. If the decision was wrong, learn from your mistakes. The four-step process of working through mistakes is (1) admit you made a mistake and accept responsibility, (2) recover, (3) put procedure into place to avoid reoccurrence, and (4) learn from it, and put it behind you. You may not always make the right decision, but you must be willing to commit to a decision.

DECISION MAKING—ACTIVITY

Personnel scenario: Jack has worked under you for a few years. His performance has been mediocre, and he has been on a performance plan. While on the plan, he did what was laid out for him without hesitation and demonstrated some improvement. On an in-service day, Jack does not show. There is no phone call to tell of his whereabouts. The next day, Jack shows up to work two hours late. When you discuss the situation with him, he states he went to the dentist's office and figured you'd be okay with this decision since he went on a day when students weren't affected. He was late the second day due to pain from the dental work and arranged with one of the teachers to take his early classes. No communication was made to you as his direct supervisor, and his actions were not preapproved.

What questions would you ask?

Who can you include in your inner circle when making a decision on handling this situation?

What might your immediate or emotional reaction look like, and how might this differ after you take the time to write out pros and cons to that decision?

Write out at least three ways this situation could be handled.

Programming scenario: Your school currently offers an Accelerated Math program. The program was recently brought to your attention by the program teacher. Her concerns range from inconsistency of performance by the students to questioning the curriculum. As the two of you meet, you realize: (1) Criteria for participation in the program has deteriorated. Rather than basing participation on the performance of the student, it is vocal parents' children who are enrolled. (2) The inconsistency of performance of the students enrolled has caused the teacher to have to slow instruction, and participants are no longer able to complete high school algebra as eighth-grade students. Therefore, it is no longer an accelerated program.

What are the goals of the program, and what needs to be done to reach these goals?

Who can you invite into your inner circle to assist with decision making?

What is the timeline for implementation of your decision?

How will parents be notified of changes within the program and how will unhappy parents be handled?

What data can you use to assist with your decision making?

DECISION MAKING—REFLECTION

Think of a decision you made where things turned out well. Who was part of that process, and how did you feel?

Think of a decision you made when things did not turn out so well. Were others involved in the decision-making process? How did you feel about the situation? How did others handle it? Did you take responsibility for the decision?

Discuss a decision you made too quickly or when the situation was too current where your decision was emotional. How could you have handled that situation differently, and how might that have changed the outcome?

Share an experience where your intuition or gut decision proved right.

13

Professional Development and Training

Administrators are key in providing professional development opportunities and training to staff within their building. Generally, professional development should be practical and relevant to the needs of the staff. Realize that attention and engagement will depend on relevancy and whether or not participants feel they can apply the professional development to their placement.

It is difficult to provide professional development for a diverse staff unless the particular training is generic to all teachers on the staff (e.g., district code of conduct and application to the classroom situation, etc.).

By providing a variation of offerings, you increase chances of success. Take into consideration the grade levels you're servicing, subject areas, and differences in roles (i.e., teachers, support staff, paraprofessionals, volunteers). Classroom teachers have a different focus than counselors, nurses, or specialists. Is your professional development reflective of this? Do you offer different sessions or breakout sessions that address the needs of each group? Asking for staff input of interests and needs can build buy-in and increase interest.

There should be a close link between theory and practice. Application of the information shared at the in-service needs to be done within days, or will most likely not take place at all.

There also needs to be follow-up of the session in order to increase the success level. A one-day session may spark some interest, answer some questions, or raise others. However, should the teachers be provided the opportunity to not only hear information, but perhaps do a literature review, have some discussions with other educators, implement, reflect, and report back about their experience of the application within their placement, you have now extended the opportunity to a real-life setting.

Professional development can also be specific in that you are the instructional leader of the school. You complete both formal and informal observations of your staff. Therefore, you are a great resource to your teacher. You can provide recommendations for areas of necessary improvement, or perhaps requirements if areas are interfering with the teacher's promise of tenure or renewal.

By being aware of the professional goals of your staff, you can serve as a resource by passing on information from area colleges or sharing mailings or faxes that directly correlate with these goals.

Training of staff should be practical in that it addresses the needs for the role(s) of the participants. It should also be flexible. As training is taking place, participants' background knowledge and experience may warrant moving through material at a faster, or slower, pace. Just as with our students, sometimes participants need us to reteach if they don't understand material.

If we want our staff to use materials, whether it be a new textbook series, software, or Smartboards, then we need to be sure we are providing training. There should be reference material provided at the training. This will assist the participant with note taking and more focus during the presentation, as well as a refresher if the information isn't applied right away.

One of the most important trainings that is often overlooked is orientation. First determine if orientation will be at the district or building level. Then identify who is responsible for the training, including communicating the times, securing the location, snacks and meals, ordering of materials, presenter notes and overheads/PowerPoints, the presenter, and needs of the presenter (LCD, screen, podium, table, etc.). Take into consideration the budget and the costs incurred. For example, is there a cost for the speaker? Is there a cost for materials? Is there a limit to the number of participants?

How is training, particularly orientation, addressed with staff who join your team mid-year? This group is often forgotten in that many times this group is thrown into duties without training or after participating in modified training. If training is modified, be sure participants have the opportunity to participate in a full training at another time. As the administrator, providing the support of a peer mentor as well as your ongoing support is essential.

Do a great job providing professional development to your staff; remember to do the same for yourself. What are your interests and your needs? Are there areas that you know are challenging for you that you can focus on for growth?

Professional development should align and support goals of the district, or more specifically, goals of the school. If you want specific outcomes, work to support your teachers by providing the professional development and training necessary to provide both foundational knowledge as well as follow-up sessions to come to the desired outcome.

PROFESSIONAL DEVELOPMENT AND TRAINING—ACTIVITY

Develop an input sheet for teachers to complete prior to the start of the school year. On the form, identify areas of interest for both trainings and professional development opportunities. For example, SMART Board, mimeoboard, MAPs, DORA, APEX, or other specified trainings. Areas of professional development may be classroom management, differentiated instruction, or development of a learning style and student interest inventory.

PROFESSIONAL DEVELOPMENT AND TRAINING—REFLECTION

What makes a good professional development session to you?

What was the focus of the last professional development session that you went to where you really left the session revitalized, energized, and eager to utilize the information you learned?

What made the session exciting to you?

With this in mind, how could you ensure the professional development you set up for your teachers will have a similar effect on them?

14

Testing and Assessment

For purposes of discussion, testing refers to tools, events, and activities which measure student progress and which identify student strengths and weaknesses. This chapter covers best practices of design and use of teacher-made tests, district-made tests, purchased tests, and state/national tests. Each of these test formats—aligned with curriculum, carefully prepared, valid and reliable, appropriately mentored to students, and thoroughly analyzed to determine student progress, strengths, and weaknesses—plays a significant role in the teaching/learning process.

The educational leader assists with the design, implementation, and use of test measurements. Mentorship flows from the leader to the teacher and then to the student. Teachers may need assistance in designing appropriate tests. Teachers and students need knowledge of the content, testing process, and appropriate analysis process of outside tests, whether district prepared, district purchased, or state/nationally mandated. Without appropriate knowledge, testing becomes just an activity of little worth.

TEACHER-CREATED TESTS

This section reviews best practices of teacher-made tests. Such tests are based on every phase of instruction. First, the teacher designs lessons based on specifically designed objectives. These objectives flow from district curriculum, which aligns with state and national curriculum expectations. The teacher's lessons, so designed, align with the established curriculum.

This all means the teacher knows the objectives and knows how to teach toward the accomplishment of the objectives. The teacher is not teaching off of personally designed objectives. The teacher is not flying blind. The principal, the district curriculum coordinator, and the district subject-area specialists share mentorship with teachers, ensuring that teachers structure their lessons according to the principles stated above. As in other situations, mentorship is intensive for new teachers and review for experienced teachers. Good mentorship never stops after the first year.

Second, the teacher designs an appropriate assessment. Guidelines for an appropriate assessment are:

- The test actually measures the extent to which the student has achieved specific objectives.
- The assessment reflects the methods used to teach.
- The assessment provides a wide variety of and subject-appropriate responses.
- The teacher prepares the students for taking the test effectively (reviewing how to prepare for the test and reviewing the format of the test).

Following the test, the teacher determines individual student progress, strengths, and weaknesses. The teachers share that information with the students. The teacher restructures lessons on the basis of information gathered. The teacher, through phone calls, parent meetings, and written communication, shares information with parents on a regular basis. All of the above makes testing a valid, useful, and meaningful experience.

DISTRICT AND STATE/NATIONAL TESTS

District-designed or -purchased tests present a major challenge right from the start. Teachers often feel a sense of detachment. Teachers may feel that the test is forced on them. Teachers may deplore the time such tests take away from instructing. Teachers may use only a small portion of available data. Teachers may feel that the post-test data is useless. The problem is that teacher detachment sends a specific message to the student: this is not really important. And the students respond accordingly.

Mentorship of district tests addresses the detachment issue. The appropriate district personnel mentor school principals. School principals mentor teachers. Most importantly, teachers carefully mentor students. Such mentorship predicts, but does not necessarily guarantee, that students will work hard on the test and provide legitimate results. Teachers also need mentoring related to the good and actual use of generated data. Finally, both leadership and mentorship merge in an annual review of the testing process and the results therefrom.

State- and national-mandated testing has the same detachment issue, perhaps more so. Preparation for the test is complex. The testing schedule is elaborate, taking away much instruction time. The intensive testing process wears students out. Motivating students to succeed is very difficult. Testing data does not come back to the teachers in an efficient, timely manner.

Despite all these challenges and the potential for low performance resulting from the challenges, the state/nation uses aggregate data to judge the performance of schools and districts. This means extensive mentoring and leading—annually. This means leading that provides teacher motivation, student motivation, and the appropriate test schedule and testing environment. All are necessary for such testing to actually measure student growth.

TESTING AND ASSESSMENT—ACTIVITY

Identify the tests/assessments that are used in your school and/or district.

Identify the purpose of each of these tests/assessments.

How is the data being used? Is there a way to improve the use?

Is the data returned to the district, school, and teacher in a timely manner?

Describe the diagnostic-prescriptive process.

How is instruction impacted by data-driven decisions?

Chapter 14

TESTING AND ASSESSMENT—REFLECTION

What is your attitude toward assessment of students? How would this affect your staff and students?

Think about your current school situation. How can you prepare your teachers and students for the tests administered? How can you support them?

What could you do in your role to assist with students who haven't "made the mark"?

15

Student Achievement

Student learning is often a function of what teacher you get, rather than what school you go to.

—R. Elmore

The single greatest factor in student achievement is teacher practice.

—R. Marzano

Poverty impacts student achievement, but instruction and leadership matter more.

—D. Reeves

Teacher and administrator expectations for student learning impact actual outcomes.

—Rosenthal and Jacobson

INVESTING IN QUALITY STAFF

When exploring what causes achievement, a theme emerges. Qualified staff are an investment in student achievement. Holding a teaching license, taking necessary state examinations, participating in alternative certification, and one's experience in the field are components that determine qualified staff by definition. While these are the documented requirements through No Child Left Behind, there are other areas to consider.

Knowledge, experience, a good attitude, energy, and a demonstrated interest in lifelong learning are areas to probe when interviewing candidates for prospective faculty or staff. Ask questions and gather information that supports the person's competence in subject matter and teaching skills.

Good teaching qualities should be evident during the interview. These qualities include the candidate's understanding of the importance of building relationships and getting to know one's students; finding the instructional level and learning styles of students both individually and within a group; continual assessment with the willingness to change instruction; maintaining high expectations for all students; and challenging all students.

Have the candidate share specific examples of being a reflective practitioner. For example, can she or he share a project that did not go well, as well as ideas about what went wrong and how she or he could correct it should she or he use that activity/lesson again?

Focused professional development and intense supervision can assist with progression of professional goals. Professional development should support goals and allow staff interaction. Building professional learning communities and the use of mentors and coaches help to support teachers. Providing teachers with resources and support and holding them accountable to demonstrate high levels of performance send a clear message from administration.

CREATING AN EFFECTIVE ENVIRONMENT

The physical environment that surrounds a child is important. From the first steps into the foyer of the school, a message is sent. A child-centered, welcoming, safe environment is the product of hard and focused work. Adults with a vested interest in the children create such an environment.

Each classroom provides an image of the teacher's style, interests, and talents. Colorful, interesting, age-appropriate, and subject-relevant material may drape the walls. Posted work celebrates the accomplishments of the students. Overstimulation and clutter should be avoided. Traffic pathways should be left open, and vents and windows should not be blocked. Natural lighting is pleasant to the eyes and has been identified as beneficial to the learner in educational research. The physical layout of the classroom can take many forms. The important thing is that it is conducive to education and follows the philosophy of the school.

Strive for balance within each classroom. Large group, small group, individual work, partners, buddies, or peer-to-peer varied grouping based on the type of activity, skill level, or interest of students can be fine-tuned when you know your students. Using random grouping occasionally is acceptable, but alignment leads to more effective classrooms.

ASSESSMENT AND USING DATA

Assessment should be ongoing. Determine methods of formal and informal assessments in which you will participate. Which assessments are mandated, and which are optional? What is the cost of these assessments? What types of data and reports can be generated?

You've taken the time to test the students. What have you done with the results? How will the results impact student achievement? Assessment to instruction requires teachers understand the process of using multiple assessments to determine the instructional level of each student, and lessons are planned with consideration of the student's strengths and weaknesses in that particular area.

FLUID CURRICULUM

It is imperative that curriculum be fluid. This means that there is open communication between teachers of all levels, and time is set aside for discussions to take place regarding skills actually taught at each grade level.

Whether the school has a curriculum director who is responsible for the overall curriculum of the district, or the principal acts as the instructional leader and facilitates the writing and implementation of the curriculum, teachers must be involved in the process. It is the teachers who are in the classrooms on a daily basis and know what is actually taking place, meaning instructional levels, amount of material, skills covered within the course of the year, and so on. What looks good to administrators on paper could be meaningless in practice; therefore, it is imperative that teachers have a voice.

If working in a K–8 district, it is important to connect with your local feeder high school(s) to ensure that the curriculum from your school to the local high school is seamless and fluid. It is easy to get caught up in the vision or focus of your particular school, but you must be cognizant of the foundation you create for your students to be successful at the next level.

MEANINGFUL PLANNING

> Intelligence is not a stable and fixed set of traits. It is a current state of being.
>
> —Reuven Feuerstein

With the above statement in mind, this means that the teacher is the instrument to providing experience, knowledge, resources, and expansions; searching for connections; and building confidence our children so desperately need to process and build their understanding. As learners, our brain seeks engagement, challenge, and feedback.

Teachers need guidance and training in creating masterful lesson plans that tend to these needs. It is one thing to put some page numbers in a block within a lesson planner; however, to create plans that engage students and are effective for learners takes thoughtful planning. Meaningful planning takes learners' instructional levels into account, with information taken from various sources: daily work, MAPs testing, standardized test scores, reading inventories, prior classroom teacher input, input from specialist teachers, and so forth.

Meaningful planning also means that one takes into account the skills that are to be taught, readiness of the students, mastery, the need for reteaching, extension activities, integration of technology, and so on.

Field trips and assemblies should be aligned with curriculum. Any media used, such as videos, should directly relate to the material. Choices are made with purpose.

ASSESSMENT, CURRICULUM, INSTRUCTION, AND PROFESSIONAL DEVELOPMENT

As an administrator, you understand the connectedness of assessment, curriculum, instruction, and professional development. This cycle demands that we look at each part to create a whole. We need to assess to understand a benchmark for each child, as well as analyze progress. We need to understand the skills that are introduced, practiced, and/or mastered at each level within the curriculum. We need to provide instruction that identifies strengths and practices weaknesses through a variety of channels within a classroom, taking individual learning styles and one's own teaching styles into account.

As one teaches or participates in observations, professional development opportunities become clear. Perhaps a formal observation reveals the teacher's struggle with classroom management, or maybe working with struggling students brings out the teacher's interest in pursuing special education coursework. Through college courses, workshops, seminars, conferences, or online opportunities, a teacher has many options to obtain or enhance knowledge in specific areas of need or interest.

PROGRAMS

With budgets that have been hard hit in many cases, administrators find themselves having to scrutinize programs, justify or defend decisions, and sometimes make cuts in programs and/or staff that can be viewed as unpopular. Special education, life skills, autism, ESL, gifted, accelerated athletics, extracurriculars such as intramurals or forensics—the programs vary but the budget calls for funds and decision making regardless of the origin of the program. Be creative and search for outside sources such as funding from federal government, state government, grants, or foundations that support educational efforts.

As stated earlier, keep in mind that all programs must be supported by the mission and vision of the school. Supported by inclusion within the strategic plan, ideas become reality and can be financially undertaken by the district.

STUDENT ACHIEVEMENT—ACTIVITY

Invite a small group of teachers to come together for a discussion on student achievement. Specifically address assessment to instruction and development of master planning. What areas need development, and how can administration and teachers work together to reach these desired outcomes?

STUDENT ACHIEVEMENT—REFLECTION

What are some areas that you feel are strengths for you? What are some areas that you feel professional development would benefit?

How does your school make decisions on programming and budget cuts? How is this information linked to student achievement?

Talk to students of varied grade levels and abilities. Find out some of their favorites and why, and how those areas could be improved (e.g., dissecting more in science class). Then discuss areas that challenge students and ideas of how to improve these areas (e.g., manipulatives in math instruction). Think about the impact of the students' recommendations and what it would take to make these happen.

16

Behavior Management

Let us begin with a definition: Behavior management means policies and procedures ensuring that student behavior impacts positively on the teaching-learning climate of the school.

Behavior management (more often called "discipline") frequently ranges near the top or at the top of many teachers' "ten things I am really concerned about in my school." More often than not, behavior management is dictated by master district/union contracts.

Most often, behavior management is prescribed in documents with titles such as "Student Code of Responsibilities and Rights." Such documents delineate the course of behavior management in schools. The prescribed course of behavior management is frequently titled "Progressive Discipline."

In application of progressive discipline, teachers follow a sequence of discipline. The sequence may include conference with student, "time out," parent contact, teacher-imposed detention, referral to counselor, and finally—referral to principal.

Then the principal applies progressive discipline with referred students. Again, the sequence may involve conference with student, principal-mandated short detention, principal-mandated long detention, in-school suspension, parent-conference suspension (which means the student stays home until the parent and principal meet for a reinstatement conference), student services suspension (for continued refusal to follow school rules or for dangerous behavior), and finally central-office suspension, which may result in expulsion.

The implied reason for progressive discipline goes something like this: "After experiencing one level of behavior management, a student will behave appropriately in fear of moving to the next level." A review of discipline interventions in any school often refutes the expectation. With few exceptions, certain students routinely cycle through the behavior-management process with little change in behavior.

Students, unfortunately, do not recognize the speeding progressive discipline that lead-foot drivers experience: the warning, the ticket, the court appearance, the license suspension, and so on. In this situation, a speeder slows down, not to drive safely, but to avoid getting pulled over. The majority of students behave quite appropriately. The majority of students have no behavior file, and if they do, it contains very few interventions. And so it goes.

Discipline usually implies punishment. Discipline becomes a power and control issue, in which a teacher and a principal exercise the power of discipline in order to control (mitigate or eliminate entirely) inappropriate student behavior.

In really bad situations, discipline defaults to the principal. Having not experienced improved behavior, or because of a gross misunderstanding of progressive discipline, a teacher will routinely refer students practicing inappropriate behavior to the office. In effect, this gets rid of the student until the principal processes the behavior referral. In effect, this process does little good.

Given all of the above, leadership results in the consequence that all school personnel having direct contact with students follow the district plan for behavior management. Mentorship refers to teaching the plan to everyone: teachers, students, parents, and anyone else in the school who has direct contact with the students.

This means that every student has a copy of the student code. This means that the principal meets with student groups at the beginning of the school year to review the student code. This means that parents also have copies of the student code. This means that inexperienced teachers receive extensive instruction in reference to the code. This means that inexperienced administrators receive instruction for understanding and application of the code.

This is a lot of in-service.

One unintended result of extensive behavior management instruction is that it tends to put behavior management, rather than improved teaching and learning, at the top of the top ten lists of teacher concerns.

Does all of this mean that a behavior management plan that uses progressive discipline is generally ineffective? It does not. Progressive discipline impacts positively, as stated, the majority of students. How can behavior management improve? In what ways can a principal lead a school to an improved behavior management program?

One might think that a principal cannot do so because of known constraints of how administration can handle situations based on the contract with the local teacher's union. However . . .

Typically, a school district assumes that the student code of conduct is the sum total of behavior management. However, the student code of conduct often has no reference, no prohibition, and no motivation to layer a positive behavior management process above the student code of conduct. Herein the principal, or the central-administrator in charge of district behavior management, has the golden opportunity to practice leadership. The principal can design and implement a program layered above the official behavior management policy.

The design and implementation for such a program looks something like this:

- Research existing programs.
- Not finding an effective existing program, design a program.
- Mentor the program.
- Diffuse the argument that "we don't have to do this because it's not in the contract."
- Implement the program.
- Monitor the program for its effectiveness or lack thereof.
- Make changes in the program as necessary.
- Continue to use the official student code as the official behavior management process, with the understanding that the new plan layers above the official plan.

An example of a program that layers above the official student code of conduct follows. It is based on the acronym ORB. It is simple in concept and requires minimal effort. The goal is to improve opportunities for teaching and learning. The objective is to cause students to reflect on, and improve if necessary, their own behavior.

O in the acronym stands for "on task." And "on task" means doing what the student is expected to do everywhere and at any time during the school day. The principle assumes that students really know what "on task" means, and they must grow to the point where they can monitor their own behavior, working toward that which is appropriate.

R stands for respect: respect for self and respect for everyone in the school.

B stands for behavior. Behavior is a word that encapsulates the pages of the student code.

The principal may design posters, with ORB highlighted on the top of the page, a design depicting an ORB, and the following text:

> A student will have a good day at Sunnyside School if he or she stays on task, treats all people with respect, and behaves appropriately. None of this is easy. You must work on it. If all students stay on task, respect all people, and behave appropriately, then all of us at Sunnyside School will have a good day.

The principal mentors the program to all staff, including assistant principals, in the first staff meeting of the school year.

Teachers display their copies of the poster prominently in their classrooms.

The principal sends copies of the poster in the summer newsletter and in every newsletter sent home during the school year.

The principal reviews the concept at an early Parent Teacher Student Association meeting.

The principal monitors and reviews the ORB concept on a regular basis.

As a new program, full effective implementation may take as many years as there are the number of years students spend in the school. This is but an example of a plan, layered on top of the official behavior management, which may motivate behavior allowing effective teaching and learning.

The conclusions of this examination of behavior management are: behavior management requires leadership in design, mentorship for effective application, ongoing assessment of the program, and a search for ways to improve the program.

BEHAVIOR MANAGEMENT—ACTIVITY

Take a walk through the school. Informally take note of what you observe. Is the behavior management plan adopted by the school in effect? Is it being practiced consistently between teachers? If not, what is your next step?

Review your student code of responsibilities and rights or whatever document would be like this in your school/district. Review your behavior management plan. Do the two complement each other? Are both in effect simultaneously?

BEHAVIOR MANAGEMENT—REFLECTION

How effective is your plan?

Are students responsive to your plan? What are you doing right? What can be improved?

Do parents support your plan? Is this an area that can be improved, and if so, how?

What do you know about your students? Do you know them by name? Do you know personal information? Interests, hobbies, what's happening in their lives? How does this correlate with behavior management?

17

Dealing with the Difficult

Using perhaps an oversimplified explanation, "difficult" falls between "routine" and "crisis." This chapter outlines procedures for administrators who must work with difficult students, teachers, other school staff, parents, and community situations.

Difficult students are those whom teachers just want to disappear—to the office, out of my class, out of our school. That's the easiest thing to do. Get rid of them and my class will be better. Get rid of them and our school will improve. Teachers with that kind of attitude basically admit that they do not want to work with students who present a challenge. However, when the problematic student leaves, a new one either enrolls or another rises to the occasion. In other words, there will always be students viewed as problematic.

Leadership can change the mindset of teachers. Mentorship teaches the process of dealing effectively with the difficult. As it turns out, schools usually have available a lengthy menu of interventions that lead to better behavior, more effective teaching/learning opportunities, better social behavior, and improved academic accomplishment.

In dealing with the difficult student, the principal and teachers must gather data, review the options available, and develop a plan for working with the student. This plan, reviewed frequently, changes as needs warrant. Ultimately, the plan helps the student mitigate whatever the challenge. The intervention options are not new creations. They include:

- Progressive discipline
- Frequent parent contact, for both academic and behavior issues
- School support team interventions
- Evaluation for special needs; design IEP if data supports such activity

- Finding the positive in each child
- Extensive written documentation, no matter what procedure is used
- Compliance with district procedures throughout
- An attitude of respect for the student and the student's challenges

It is not the intention of this discourse to explain and to give examples of each of the interventions and procedures. Rather, the intent is to state that teachers, principal, support staff, and parents must consider all possible options and must remember to review the established plan and modify it if necessary. In dealing with the difficult, there are no quick fixes.

In the shadowy reaches, deep within school culture, teachers and other staff may cause difficulties. Options for dealing with such staff are again well known. The principal must commit time and must consider various options for working with difficult staff.

Again, there is no quick fix. Following constraints of the district/union contract, thorough investigation, specific written documentation, application of due process, and using the progressive discipline outline for teachers—all are steps in the process. The district and the principal cannot confront a teacher regarding inappropriate behaviors abruptly and without investigation.

The master contract may prescribe progressive discipline for teachers and other staff. In each step of progressive discipline, the contract may require union representation. The process: informal conference with no written documentation in the teacher's file; reprimand conference with a reprimand letter placed in the teacher's file; hearing before the district human resources director; written reprimand from the HR director; suspension from duties issued by the HR director; hearing for termination, perhaps involving the board of education.

The intent of the progressive discipline process is to change teacher behavior. If the behavior does not change, the discipline moves further up the ladder. Anyone who has followed this procedure will say that it is uncomfortable, challenging, and time consuming. Also, anyone who has followed this procedure will state that he or she operates under a microscope, as the union and the district watch closely. It's not fun.

Parents may cause trouble. They may enable their children by denying inappropriate behavior, by complaining about the discipline of their children, by making demands of the principal, by showing up at school unannounced and raising a verbal fuss in the office and in the school hallways. The list of examples goes on.

Without appearing to be redundant, to work effectively with a difficult parent, follow a pre-established plan. Treat the parent with respect. The principal is the professional. Getting defensive or angry does nothing to solve the problem; instead, such behavior intensifies the problem. Attempt to define the parent's concern. Propose methods for resolving the concern. Document. Document. Document.

Advise central administration about the issues if they continue unresolved. The parent, unappreciative of the principal's activities, may run over to see the superintendent or the principal's direct supervisor. The supervisor needs to know that the parent is coming over and why.

If the parent puts anyone in the school at risk, involve school security. If the parent behavior goes beyond the ability of school security to resolve it, involve law enforcement. Again, have a plan, follow it, document everything, and notify your boss.

If the school district has a parent complaint procedure and the parent issues a written complaint, follow district procedure. Time and date receipt of the complaint. Respond to the complaint citing district procedure and by reviewing the documents outlining how the principal has worked with the student. Conclude by stating the complaint does not have merit or does have merit. If the complaint is in any way valid, outline a plan for working with the student and parent.

Difficult situations in the community may impact the school. Again, the principal follows a plan. Get as much information as you can. For example, a police scanner running in the office can provide information to which you can be proactive instead of reactive (e.g., a traffic incident blocking a major intersection). A phone call to transportation can allow reroute of the school buses over delay. Make every effort to keep business as usual in the school.

Advise teachers about what is going on. Word spreads quickly. To avoid rumors, which frequently get worse as they are passed along, a confidential written memo or even an all-school announcement helps to tell the real story. The intent is not to alarm anyone in the school but to communicate accurate information.

If the outside situation is very serious, implement the school crisis response plan. The process itself is simple: assess the situation and follow a pre-established plan. In no situation does a principal want to make up a response as the situation develops but that must occur. A principal needs to think quickly, to make a quick mental review of existing plans, and to make decisions about what aspects of a plan to implement.

Finally, though it may be very difficult, the principal must set the tone of calmness and confidence before the school. Panic and uncertainty breed panic.

Reflecting on the above situations, there is one common element: follow a pre-established plan. Leadership is designing the plans and implementing them if necessary. Mentorship is teaching the plans to those who need to know what the elements of the plan are and how to implement them. Such planning, mentoring, and implanting promote an effective school climate, where teaching and learning occur and where everybody in the school is safe and secure.

DEALING WITH THE DIFFICULT—ACTIVITY

Think about the following situations. Write down how you respond to each. Discuss them with your mentor.

(1) You have a colleague who is equal to you in reporting. The person is insanely jealous of you, and perhaps your success in your position is intimidating to her. Rather than work toward goals of her own, she chooses to put you down to other people. Since you are well respected, others come to you and report what this colleague is saying.

(2) You tell a parent that she needs to attend a field trip to chaperone her own child. The parent attends the trip and is just as bad, if not worse, than the child regarding behavior.

(3) A board member joined with a focused agenda of her own. Every meeting has her topic of interest woven into it. While others try to redirect her, she continues to push her agenda in any forum and in any way she can.

(4) A student is bullying another student. You are aware of it but cannot catch the student in action. She sends a message "telephone style" through the classroom that she's going to beat the student up, giving a time and location, but then denies she said this. She kicks the student while changing books at the locker. She wears consequences like a badge, then smirks and motions to the other child that she's going to get her.

DEALING WITH THE DIFFICULT—REFLECTION

How do you handle it when someone confronts you unexpectedly? Are you quiet? Defensive? Vocal? Explain how you handle the situation.

Taking the prior question into consideration, talk with your mentor to gain insight into changes that may be recommended in how you handle confrontation.

Do you handle difficult people differently? If so, how and why?

18

Communication

TRUST

Trust requires self-disclosure. This means sharing your failures, acknowledging challenges, celebrating successes, and dreaming dreams. It means listening to others and not always offering answers or sharing your stories. It means being trustworthy, having an open door and a closed mouth with confidential matters. Trust means nonjudgmental guidance and no retaliation when there's a disagreement. Positive attitude and compliments both directly in front of the person as well as to others in earshot of the person help to build trust.

VERBAL VS. NONVERBAL COMMUNICATION

It is said that as much as 95 percent of communication is nonverbal. Nonverbal messages such as eye contact, facial expressions, placement of hands, or posture can tell you how someone is feeling in a situation. Reading, understanding, and responding to the person on the edge of his or her seat and leaning forward in interest or sitting back rubbing his or her neck in frustration is nonverbal communication.

Understanding nonverbal cues can assist when working with people; however, you must also gain an understanding of cultural and religious differences as well as taking life situations into account. For example, looking away to break eye contact or covering one's mouth when speaking can be cues for covering up a lie. However, eye contact to a position of authority is a sign of disrespect in some cultures, or a person may be self-conscious and cover his or her mouth if dental work had just been performed (or needs to be performed).

Verbal communication is most effective when precise language is used. Share information in a way that people can understand, meaning leave out the jargon.

Don't talk down to people, and speak in simple terms. Articulation is important, as is the choice of words. In many situations, it is not what you say but how you say it. Speak directly to parties involved, as it is demoralizing to hear information from outside sources when it directly relates to you.

Communicating clearly and effectively can be a determining factor for promotion. Getting your message across, whether verbally or in writing, is essential in administration. You must understand the message, your audience, and how your message may be perceived, taking into consideration situational and cultural context. You must share your information with confidence that it is useful and accurate. Most importantly, your message must be interpreted correctly by recipients.

Lack of information, misinterpretation, misunderstanding, or emotional reactions are all barriers to communication. Consideration of the length, organization, and accuracy of the message with relation to the culture and knowledge of the topic of discussion is a way to increase successful communication.

Finally, determination of the vehicle of communication with regard to the message and audience is imperative. Should you share the message in person, by telephone, or via e-mail? Should you invite a third party? When and where should we meet? How much time will this take if we approach the topic and leave time for discussion and questions so we are both on the same page? Is this a situation where body language or intonation can assist with interpretation of the message?

DEALING WITH THE DIFFICULT

When you feel that you are entering a meeting that could be difficult, you have to make a difficult phone call, or you see a parent or staff member coming your way with a look of vengeance, there are some things that you can do. Think about the relationship you have with that person. If you have had the opportunity to build rapport with him or her, then capitalize on this as you deal with the difficult. Determine areas that you can focus on in a positive light. Take a pulse on where you are with the situation, asking yourself what's important to you as you head into the situation.

Take time to listen—attentively. Do not think about what you'll say next or how to defend yourself, but truly listen. Provide a setting where you can focus on the concerns—not in a hallway. Once you are in a good environment to talk, utilize good communication skills such as eye contact, body language, summarizing what you've heard, being reflective, and listening without interruption. The use of "I" statements share feelings without fault or putting a person on the defense. An example of an "I" statement is "I feel . . . when you . . . because . . . and I need . . ." Keep in mind that you cannot rationalize an irrational person.

An important piece is that you need to be accountable, and if the situation warrants, you need to be able to say you're wrong. There are a lot of emotions that can surface when differences are expressed. Watch the defensiveness, and be sure not to talk down to people. Remember that you have something in common—the children.

Be proactive. If you think there may be a problem, face it head on. Contact the parent or make an appointment with the staff member before the issues are magnified and tempers flare.

Keep in mind that it's the words you choose that make a difference. Choose words that shed a positive light as your choice of words do make a difference in how people process the information. For example, inviting a parent to the school to discuss their child's progress is seen in a more positive light than summoning them to come to discuss their child's failing grades.

SHARING THE VISION

Leaders are charged with the responsibility to be the conduit of change. Change can bring about many different emotions. Some people despise change and are happy with the way things are, or would rather have things status quo and familiar than to face the unknown. Then there are those who welcome change as a catalyst of growth.

We know change is necessary. Think about some common sayings you have heard regarding change. For example, doing things the same way multiple times does not render a different outcome, or the only difference between a rut and a grave is the depth of the hole.

When change is warranted, research, communicate, and work for buy-in. Brainstorm and generate ideas reflective of multiple perspectives. Remove unsatisfactory or unfeasible ideas from the mix. Organize the ideas and explore the alternatives. Determine implications for each suggestion through research and analysis, and validate that the idea is reflective of the objective. Determine participants in the decision-making process, and provide time for discussion and questions. Several eyes on documents, ears in meetings, and mouths discussing the ideas ensure the process has been well thought-out and errors have been identified. Implications and assumptions are reviewed as a group. Risks and benefits have been determined and support the decision.

COMMUNICATION—ACTIVITY

Take the time to role-play these scenarios with your mentor. As the administrator, remember that the content needs to be accurate and specific; the form should show effective organization; the impact of the meeting should evidence problem solving with a clear message conveyed to all parties; the process should be effective; and the presentation should be professional.

Role play #1: You are heading into a meeting with an irate parent. You invited her to come in for a meeting because she was raising her voice to you on the phone and you figured it was best to address the situation in person. Ms. Green feels that you are targeting her daughter, Heather, who has done nothing to warrant your behavior toward her.

Role play #2: You provide a formal observation on veteran staff member Barbara Flugglebinder. She is unhappy with your input since she has so many years of experience—in fact, you were probably still in diapers when she started teaching. She questions how you can have anything to contribute to her career, since she has gone unchallenged throughout her years at ABC School where the parents and students all love her. Barbara has an appointment with you in two days, but in the meantime she has been toxic in the faculty lounge.

Role play #3: Mr. Jackson catches you in the hallway. He is furious that the coach didn't play his son, Brett, in the basketball game on Saturday. If his son would've been played, the team would have won.

Role play #4: Mrs. Smith approaches you at student pick-up while you are directing cars, buses, and pedestrians. She states that one of her daughter's friends keeps posting mean things about her on her Facebook wall.

COMMUNICATION—REFLECTION

Reflect upon a situation you encountered between you and a parent or staff member. Think about the encounter through these questions:

What are the possible benefits of effective communication?

What questions might you have left unanswered?

Why would it be important to know what someone knows, thinks, and believes as you head into a meeting?

How would you feel if you were walking in this person's shoes?

19

Walk-Throughs

The walk-through serves as an effective tool to assist the principal in knowing what is happening in the school. The teachers union and the district master contract state specifically what process the administration must use for teacher evaluation, and sometimes the walk-through may cause worry and concern. An administrator cannot, according to the contract, use anything noticed and observed during a walk-through as part of the evaluation process. A walk-through should not be done with the intent of evaluation.

The walk-through can be described as a quick unscheduled drop-in on teaching sessions for the purposes of a snapshot of teaching and learning activity, to observe and acknowledge special projects, to show respect for teaching and learning, and to maintain visibility and connection with students and teachers. The caveat again: the walk-through is not and cannot be part of the evaluation process.

The school principal must prepare the staff and students for the walk-through process. The definition should appear in the summer staff bulletin and parent newsletter. The principal must remind staff that the walk-through is not a covert evaluation.

While the walk-through process may cause anxiety at its inception, teachers and students alike will soon appreciate the process. Should a walk-through surface concerns, the administrator must use the teacher evaluation system to address the concerns.

As an introduction to the process, in the first walk-through of the school year, the principal can introduce himself or herself, make general positive comments about the school, tell the students his or her office door is open to any student at any time, and answer questions from students.

Set the guidelines of your future visits. The teachers should know that you are not there to interrupt the educational process so they should continue teaching. Students should know it is not a time to wave, talk to you, or tattle on a classmate. It is simply your time with them. Both students and teachers appreciate this initial visit. In a middle school or high school level, there may be a lot of homerooms where this initial visit may take some additional time.

You may wish to implement a system dependent on the structure of your district/school, such as visiting all kindergarten, sixth grade, or freshmen during the first period on the first day of school. For those new to the school, this is a great way to introduce oneself, share your open door policy, and answer questions, the most popular of which is typically "When's lunch?" It also begins the process of building rapport and putting names with faces to get to know each student by name.

As a principal, make it a priority to find good activities in the school and to support them regularly. Make regular visits to exploratory classes. Stop in to listen to the band, or watch part of a play rehearsal. Observe teaching and learning activities throughout the school.

By implementing a consistent walk-through program, you develop a very clear picture of the good teaching/learning processes going on daily. It can give insight as to teaching styles and effective classroom management and provide firsthand experience that you can share with parents as you speak with them about their children or what's happening in their child's classroom.

Often you develop mutual respect of students, teachers, and parents. The walk-throughs are evidence of the principal showing interest, having a presence, and being actively involved. Walk-throughs give administrators the opportunity to see what is truly going on in the classrooms on a daily basis; the nuts and bolts of instruction without dog and pony shows.

As in many school situations, leadership by example works best. For a brand new administrator, the walk-along process, followed by a debriefing, is very effective for walk-through process. To fit this experience into mentoring, it often begins prior to the start of the school year with a "Read This" session as the new administrator reads the "Walk-Through" article in the summer staff bulletin. A "Listen to Me" session follows, as you and your new administrator begin the walk-through process. And, as stated above, the "Walk with Me" introduces the new administrator to the process.

Over the years, the walk-through process becomes something you are known to do and it is appreciated by teachers, students, and parents. Taking that daily walk through the school builds a connection and rapport, increases understanding of what is actually taking place within one's building, and builds mutual respect.

WALK-THROUGH—ACTIVITIES

Design a program of walk-throughs for you and your school.

Draft the article about walk-throughs that you will send to your teachers and parents in the summer bulletins.

Discuss with your mentor the process you will use to implement the walk-through.

Implement the walk-through process on the first day of school.

Make time for the walk-through process on a regular basis.

WALK-THROUGH—REFLECTION

As you return to your office the first few weeks of your walk-through experience, jot down some of the observations you made, such as great teaching strategies in place, projects where students really had the opportunity to demonstrate learning, and such. Don't necessarily write down names, and don't do it while you are in the classroom or teachers may feel they are being evaluated. After a few weeks, review your list. What are your thoughts? What stands out to you?

20

Staff Observations and Evaluations

Simply put, the observation process depends entirely on specific and relative district, local board, and/or union contract language. Given that, leaders do not design observation procedures that meet the needs of the individual school or the observation style of the principal.

Given the restrictions noted here, leadership does not develop objectives or programs. The master contract addresses both. Instead, the effective leader understands the evaluation process, mentors properly, and implements it totally.

Implementation takes certain steps. First, the leader/principal in an annual review mentors the observation and evaluation process to experienced staff, especially if new contract language calls for changes. A staff meeting early in the year prior to the principal observing and evaluating teachers is a good venue for this process.

Second, the principal mentors new staff with precise instruction about the whole process. A staff meeting for new teachers early in the year serves to mentor new teachers.

Third, the principal communicates effectively with all teachers. The principal must advise, most likely through the use of written memos to each individual, which teachers are up for review in the school year. Many master contracts for new teachers call for completion of the whole observation and evaluation by the end of the first semester. Some district contracts call for a first semester evaluation with goals and objectives outlined for the second or third evaluation based upon observations from the initial or preceding observation. Experienced teachers also need to know the tentative schedule for their observation and evaluation.

Both experienced and new teachers need to know what they will be evaluated on and their designated evaluator. Pre-evaluation conferences serve to outline lesson focus and demonstrate teaching/learning goals. When school administration consists of a directing principal and one or more assistant principals, it is particularly important that the teachers know which administrator has been identified to conduct their evaluation.

The evaluator must schedule the meeting date and time for the pre-observation conference, the time or times for the actual observations, and the date and time for the post-observation conference. The evaluator must also schedule a meeting for discussion of the final prepared evaluation document. Facilitating the observation and evaluation process effectively requires sticking to such schedules precisely. Teachers find being stood up offensive.

Finally, effective leadership means sticking to the plan. A principal must not, for any reason, attempt circumventing the prescribed evaluation process. If a principal cuts a break for an experienced teacher ("We'll just skip your evaluation this year," for example), other teachers will find out about the deal. Such behavior causes the teachers union to file grievances. Principals are bound by the contract and may not deviate from such an important step in the process.

Effective mentorship for new principals requires a more detailed process. If a new principal is a stand-alone in a school, completely effective mentorship comes from an experienced principal from another school. This is also the process to follow if the new principal serves as directing principal, with one or more assistant principals. The directing principal serves as mentor for inexperienced assistant principals.

First, the mentor uses the "Listen to Me" mentoring procedure. The new principal must learn the specific district/board/union contract language. The new principal must also learn the process that the district implements using the procedures described in the contract language. Instead of using another principal or the directing principal for this aspect of mentoring, the district could schedule a workshop for all new principals and assistant principals, with one district principal serving as the teacher. If the district has a significant number of new administrators in a given year, the workshop is definitely the best venue.

Second, the mentor uses the "Walk with Me" mentoring procedure. This simply means that the mentor walks the new administrator completely through one evaluation. The mentor has the new administrator sit in during each observation/evaluation activity: the pre-observation conference, the actual observation, the drafting of evaluation documents, and the post observation. In each of these activities, the mentor and new administrator debrief and review what has happened.

For this mentorship to work, the mentor must approach an experienced and effective teacher and ask that teacher to allow the new administrator to sit in. At this point, the mentor must advise the teacher that the new administrator will not contribute to the evaluation, just observe the process. In fact, the mentor may need permission from central administration and the union to mentor in this way.

Finally, as the new administrator begins the evaluation, the mentor reviews and critiques each portion of the process. The new administrator is given the reins as the veteran becomes a guide on the side.

This mentorship procedure is intensive with mentorship activities throughout the school year. The process takes a lot of time. But, effectively implemented, it works and guides a new administrator to become a good evaluator.

Leadership and mentorship come into play in situations where teachers evaluate educational assistants whom they supervise. The lead engineer often evaluates the custodial staff under his supervision. In these cases, the directing principal has the leadership and mentorship responsibilities of working through the process with new staff. The teacher must understand the evaluation responsibility. The teacher must know how to use the evaluation document. The teacher must respect timelines.

Lead engineers should get evaluation in-service from the director of buildings and grounds. However, this responsibility may default to the building principals.

In both cases, responsibility for effective evaluations belongs, ultimately, to the directing principal. Effective leadership and mentorship make the evaluation of educational assistants and building custodians effective.

OBSERVATION AND EVALUATION—ACTIVITY

Read the following scenarios. Write down your thoughts on how you would deal with each situation. Think about your role in coaching your teachers. Discuss your thoughts with your mentor.

(1) You have a teacher whose performance has progressively gotten worse over the past three years. As you are mentored into the position, you are made aware that instruction has taken a plunge. The teacher looks to be ineffective from test data, and parents are complaining that the teacher does not challenge the students and is unprepared with lessons. From conversations with the teacher, you know that she is a single parent dealing with some issues with her teenage daughter and some health concerns of her own.

(2) A veteran teacher, well respected and an icon in the community, is unwilling to follow district goals of implementing technology in the classroom. This person's idea of technology is an electric typewriter. Your school offers mobile laptop labs, Podcasts, blogging, and many applications that could supplement the subject matter in a fabulous way. He refuses to use the district webgrader or student data system.

(3) Two kindergarten classes are housed across the hallway from each other. One has a teacher who is vibrant and offers a lot of movement, and students love both the activities and the teacher. While the other teacher is not a bad teacher and receives satisfactory evaluations, there is definitely a difference in teaching style. Parents have come in droves to request one teacher over the other.

OBSERVATION AND EVALUATION—REFLECTION

How do you begin the post-conference portion of the evaluation? Do you ask teachers how they feel the lesson went, and what they would change if they could? Do you jump right in and begin going over the document? What are your thoughts about this?

Do you believe in giving the highest mark on an evaluation? Can people exceed expectations? Is the evaluation written in a way that is meaningful?

What kind of specific feedback do you crave from your supervisor? In what ways is that information shared with you? How is this carried over to your meetings with your teachers?

21

Unions and Contracts

INTERVIEWING CANDIDATES

The interview is important for both you and the candidate. For you, there is a small window of opportunity to get to know as much about the person as possible. Within a short time frame you will need to assess the person not just based on whether or not they could competently complete the job duties, but other areas viewed as important for this particular role: team player, communication, motivation, catching on to new information quickly, or fitting in with the school or district.

While you are looking for these qualities, the candidate is (or should be) asking questions and gathering information to determine if this is a good fit for them, evaluating qualities such as salary, benefits, professional development, tuition reimbursement, environment, and overall job satisfaction.

During the interview, ask questions that draw out behavioral situations, such as teamwork or flexibility. Also ask situational questions that draw answers on how they might address specifics on the job, such as an irate parent or for what reasons and how she or he communicates with parents. Asking a variety of questions will help you build a team that has diverse ideas, talents, and backgrounds.

One interview method used effectively to determine the candidate's ability to organize thoughts into logical sequence is the STAR process. The interviewer asks the candidate to recall a time or situation where he or she had to deal with a particular issue—discipline, parent conference, and so on. The objective is for the candidate to: (1) describe the **S**ituation, (2) define the **T**ask, (3) list the **A**ction taken, and (4) determine **R**esults. Another format used is EAR: (1) **E**xplain the situation, (2) describe the **A**ction(s) you took, and (3) describe the **R**esults. A successful interview will have the interviewed drawing on past experiences to predict possible future behavior and success.

Each district has its own hiring practices. Hopefully, as an administrator, you will have a say as to who is hired, especially within your building. Take this charge seriously as the process to rid oneself of a problematic or unproductive employee can be long and time consuming.

Determine the criteria for which candidates would be offered an interview. Do the initial resume and even telephone screenings. If you have an HR department, they may do this for you.

You will also need to determine who sets up the interviews and who will be included in on them. If a panel or search committee is put together, determine the roles of the participants: principal, superintendent, parents, teachers, department chairs, and so forth. Review calendars to determine when interviews will be held, and then book the room(s). There should be no interruptions during the scheduled interviews, so be sure all cell phones are off (both calls and texting) and there is enough time in between interviews so you don't have to rush or have candidates stacking up.

Ask all candidates the same questions, the same way. Take notes. This will help when comparing candidates, especially if there are a few that interviewed well and you want to review responses. It also provides a legal basis that candidates are treated in a nondiscriminatory way. Having more than one person on the interview provides a look at the candidate through different lenses.

At the end of the interview, open it up to the candidate to ask questions. The types of questions asked can also give you insight as to the person's motivation for changing jobs, professional goals, or overall fit within the school/district. Give the person a time line regarding how long interviews will continue, next steps, and the anticipated fill date for the position.

An offer to the candidate of choice should take place within the proper channels of your school/district. The offer conversation can include information on the specific position as well as salary, benefits, start date, training, and orientation. Candidates not chosen should receive a letter that reflects respect and allows the candidate to keep his or her dignity.

NONRENEWAL OR TERMINATION

Nonrenewal or termination of an employee should be a last resort. From the employee perspective, the job is the person's livelihood and should be taken seriously. From the employer perspective, the employee needs to display competence and good work habits. Replacement of an employee is costly on several levels: running ads, time interviewing, paperwork, and training.

As the person's immediate supervisor, be sure to offer support. This may be through avenues such as mentoring where the teacher has a peer to discuss issues and work on general performance, or through coaching where specific areas are targeted for improvement and strategies are provided for implementation. In addition, be sure your direct reports have the training and resources they need to perform their job successfully. Retraining in targeted areas may be necessary.

If you have an HR department, work closely with them to follow procedures. Performance can be tracked through such documents as formal observations, performance appraisals, performance improvement plans, and verbal or written warnings. Be sure to follow the procedures and keep necessary documentation, as termination or nonrenewal can easily become a legal issue.

COMMON FOCUS OF UNION CONTRACTS

Collective bargaining or areas of negotiation for unions cross a broad perspective. Usually there are areas such as hiring and appointments that focus on how positions are filled, interviewing, certification, and seniority. Temporary appointments are covered, such as a person covering a position at a different level of pay or covering for another position during prep periods. Performance evaluation objectives and process, hours of work, stipends, training and professional development, observance and pay for holidays, vacation leave, sick leave, personal days, job-sharing, family and medical leave, child care emergencies, jury duty, government service, and other types of leaves are covered.

School safety, provision of a substance-free workplace, parking, commuting between buildings, licensure and certification, volunteer workers, and resignation or abandonment of a position are included. Conduct both on and off the job, disciplinary procedures, grievance procedures, legal defense, employee assistance programs, personnel files, and reasonable accommodations are covered.

Layoff and recall, management rights, union-district communication, duties of the union, and dues are included. Compensation, classification, health care, and other benefits are covered. Employee lounge, strikes, and the offering of contracts are also included.

SUPERVISORY RESPONSIBILITIES

For those who have been in a unionized environment, it is not uncommon to observe the "march of the lemons." This means that teachers who are ineffective or of poor quality are often passed on from school to school within a district. From an employee perspective, he or she still has a job. From a parent or student perspective, one needs to question the quality of education and impact that a year of ineffective teaching can have on a student, particularly if compounded by multiple years of "protected" ineffective teaching. From the administrator's perspective, consider the additional work it takes to supervise a struggling teacher and that teacher's willingness to accept redirection.

In the *Baltimore Sun*, the article "Raise city teacher pay, dismiss poor performers: National group recommends changes to union contract, state law" (Bowie, 2010) ran. This article challenges the process of dismissing poor performers. It states, "In a report released today, the National Council on Teacher Quality concludes that weak teachers are too often passed around, rather than being removed from the system. Only 14 tenured and 46 non-tenured teachers were dismissed last year from a workforce of 6,000." The article goes on to state, "The council praises the city for the amount of choice it gives principals in making hires, but says that excess teachers, even tenured ones, should be let go after a year if no principal wants them."

This is not a situation exclusive to Baltimore. Nor is it a situation exclusive to teachers, as many times administrators are protected in the same manner.

This is not to say that unions don't have a place. For those who have taught through the '60s and '70s, the unions had an instrumental role in wages, benefits, schedules, and teaching environments. The question lies in where to draw the line between protection from injustices and protection unjustly.

In a situation where one is supervising teachers who are not affiliated with a union, there is more leniency in the system to rid the school or district of an ineffective teacher; however, keep in mind that a union offers legal representation to its members whereas a person in a nonunionized environment could still sue, just on their own.

This raises the most important question, common between unionized or nonunion situations, and that is the process in place. It is the administration's responsibility to articulate the expectations, to communicate the procedure of observations or appraisals, to coach and/or mentor, and to provide a support system with the necessary resources for the teacher to succeed. If the teacher exhibits difficulties, it is the administrator's responsibility to provide an improvement plan with specifics of behavioral changes and supportive resources to bring the employee to the required level of performance.

It is also the administrator's responsibility to assist the employee in changing levels, perhaps schools, to ensure the teacher has been given every opportunity to succeed. If all of this lies on the administrator, then when the process has expired, should it not also be up to the administrator to alleviate the school or district from ineffective teaching?

GRIEVANCES

Work to understand the local protocols and limitations of your participation in events such as grievances. If a grievance is filed by the union for a teacher in your building, what is the usual modus operandi? Can you try to settle the dispute on your own? At what point does the district superintendent or board attorney become involved? What is your role at the hearing?

Perhaps the district wants you to only listen and document the concerns, and a written response to the union would be composed by the district attorney. Perhaps an objective eye needs to determine if it is an issue that can be resolved. The important piece is that the district needs to provide the mentoring and coaching necessary for the administrator to be prepared and understand the boundaries of the position so she or he does not cause bigger problems for her- or himself or the district.

WORKING WITH YOUR UNION

Districts vary in their approaches to handling union issues, so it is vital for administrators to understand this piece of their administrative role. Depending on your role, you may be required to work with a local union to negotiate teacher contracts, calendars, benefits, arbitration, and such.

With shrinking financial resources, allocations based on enrollment, changes in local economies causing mobility as people search for jobs, aging facilities, and such that play in to placement of personnel, it has become more challenging for administrators to keep positive relations with their local union. Open communication and establishing good rapport early on can help when situations get heated or ugly. In most of the larger school districts, there is an officer within central administration who works with the union and contracts; therefore, individual principals don't negotiate contracts unless appointed by the district to represent a level of schools—elementary, middle schools, high schools, and so on.

Get to know what's important to teachers, support staff, paraprofessionals, and others in your district. Understand costs, have discussions about projected changes early on, and utilize your district attorney.

I posed the question, "What do you think are the most important characteristics for new administrators that would enhance the relationship between the district and the union?" Mary Bell from Wisconsin Education Association Council offered:

> The union . . . seeks at least two things from administration in having a healthy relationship: one, that the perspective, qualifications, experience, and opinions of

educators and their representatives be sought and given due consideration in good times and in difficult times as well; and two, that administration provide the union (and the union to the administration in return) an opportunity to offer opinions and background about issues and incidents before public declarations or actions are taken. These two things demonstrate a respect for the employee representatives and the contract as well as the union respect for the rights and obligations of district administrators.

UNIONS AND CONTRACTS—ACTIVITY

Talk to your mentor and other key people regarding the union. What is the involvement of the union and/or National Education Association within the district? Do the teachers strongly support the union? What is the relationship like between the union and the district? What is important to the teachers that they are asking for support from the union?

Is it feasible in your district to make an appointment with union leadership? If so, take the time to meet with them and build a relationship outside of the negotiation table.

Locate and meet building leadership. Demonstrate your eagerness to share in open communication so misunderstandings or disagreements with decision making don't end up in grievances.

UNIONS AND CONTRACTS—REFLECTION

What are your true inner thoughts about unions? With this in mind, how can your feelings impact your relationship with your local union?

What were your expectations as a teacher? Did you rely on union support, and in what way(s)? How does that relate to your current role?

Have you terminated an employee before? Was there resistance or recourse? How did you document and prepare the employee for termination? How did you support the employee prior to making the decision to terminate? Did you consider this is the person's livelihood?

22

Recognizing Accomplishments

This chapter develops the theme of improving the recognition of students and staff through effective leadership and mentorship.

A LOOK AT PROGRAMS ALREADY IN PLACE—RECOGNITION OF STUDENTS

A basic assumption: most school districts already have in place good recognition programs. The first example: The quarterly honor roll. The school submits to the local newspaper a list of names of students achieving honors each quarter. The newspaper publishes the names under the name of the school and the headline "First Quarter Honors." Perhaps the student's homeroom or classroom teacher hands out first-quarter recognition certificates. Perhaps the school administrator makes announcements recognizing the students. Perhaps the school hosts an assembly, mainly for the students with maybe some parents in the audience. At the middle or high school levels, the grade-level counselors give certificates to the students. Being just a quarterly honor roll, the school and the district do not necessarily make a big deal out of the recognition.

The second example is district honors, recognizing students who, through the first three quarters, have maintained the "A" level grade point. This is the official school-year honor roll. The recognition process follows that of the quarterly honor recognition; however, the recognition has more significance. The program is usually held in the evening. Parents receive specific invitations to attend, and most parents do. The media coverage is more intense. Perhaps a local television station develops a news story with some footage of the program. The students receive the official district, maybe state, certificate, with the principal's and perhaps the district superintendent's signature affixed. Recognition of district honors carries significance and prestige. It's a great way to culminate a school year.

The third example is athletic awards. As the athletic program often gets more parental involvement and more media attention (both live radio/television coverage of games and more newspaper articles and photographs) than academic recognition, athletic recognition carries more importance and prestige than does the honor roll. Schools have preseason assemblies, announcing the team members. Pep assemblies precede games. Homecoming attracts a lot of attention, from the Thursday bonfire, the Friday pep assembly, the "big game," and the Saturday dance. Then the athletes get postseason glory. Good athletes and schools with a winning season receive endless media hype. All of these recognitions have merit, giving recognition to athletes and the athletic program.

The fourth example is the senior graduation program. The names of graduates appear in the newspaper. Articles and photos feature scholarship winners. The graduation ceremony is rehearsed. The audience packs the auditorium. The event—processional, speech from the principal, speech from prominent alum, speech from the valedictorian, the presenting of the diplomas, the throwing of the graduation caps—effectively ends the high school experience and points the graduates into the future.

The principal provides leadership. The leadership helps the recognitions to succeed. The leadership helps the programs to recognize what they are supposed to recognize, as opposed to a baseball coach's endless recognition of the team's state championship given during the graduation ceremony. The leadership includes close liaison between the principal and those staff actually responsible for the recognition programs. The leadership works with all parties to devise methods of improving the recognition activities. "The way we always did it" may indeed be the pinnacle of effectiveness; however, looking at the program and thinking about ways to improve it makes good sense.

EXPANDING STUDENT RECOGNITION: NEW OR SIGNIFICANTLY IMPROVED PROGRAM

A true story: A high school student asks to see her sub-school principal. The sub-school principal invites her in to his office. He asks, "What can I do for you?" The student replies, "Nothing, really. I just want to tell you that you guys don't really care about us." The sub-school principal asks, "What do you mean?" The student says, "You spend all your time working with the troublemakers and the smart kids. You don't pay any attention to kids in the middle." The principal thinks about it and says, "You are right."

The principal thinks things over. He realizes that the greater number of students in the high school do fall into the unrecognized middle group. They come to school. They attend classes. They stay out of trouble. They go to their after-school jobs. They do their homework day after day. They don't make honor roll. They do not come to the office with referrals. They don't see their counselors about getting college scholarships. They're doing the best they can. But no one pays attention to them.

This should not happen. School principals should adopt the goal of recognizing students in other ways different from honor roll and athletic glorification, recognizing students who fly under the radar, but in reality, fly and get to their destination—graduation. The objective becomes designing new recognition programs and mentoring the implementation of those programs to the faculty, to the students, and to the parents.

In designing new recognition programs, principals must be aware of one major challenge: not to develop programs that merely provide another way of recognizing students who already receive recognition. It sounds bad, but the principal must design programs that actually stay away from the honor roll students and the athletic heroes.

This means designing programs to recognize the students who fly under the radar. This means diversifying the recognition process. This means spreading the recognition process around to include the students who live from day to day with no one paying any real attention to them. The principal must, however, not design an artificially contrived program, in which students receive recognition just for the sake of getting it.

An example of such a program that may, and likely does, exist in many schools: the Student of the Month program. If the program exists, the principal must examine it carefully to make sure that it does not re-recognize students who always get honored in various ways.

The basic design of the program calls for teachers to nominate a student because she or he has made a specific impression. The teacher must consider all students with whom she or he has contact. This causes teachers to look for positives in all students. This motivates teachers of special needs students to look for accomplishments that their students make. Therein lies an excellent example of a diversity-designed program.

Careful design and implementation of a Student of the Month program make several things happen. The kids flying under the radar get recognition they never thought they would get. Such students develop the genuine feeling that they really belong to the school, and that people care about them. Parents take a new look at their kids, realizing that the kids really are doing good things.

The Student of the Month program needs a design that will make it a "big deal" in the school. Examples of possible best practices follow. Counselors run the program. It calls to their attention the worth of the under-the-radar students. This keeps the principal intimidation factor away from the program. Teachers receive written notification to nominate a student for recognition in the program. Teachers may use any personal criteria to make the nomination and may change the personal criteria throughout the school year. The counselors prepare the list of Students of the Month.

The principal schedules the program, possibly doing a program for each grade level and likely holding the program during the school day. Counselors notify students of their nomination. The principal sends a written invitation to parents, encouraging them to attend the program. The principal sends a list of students to all teachers, mandating that they allow the students to attend the program.

The principal emcees the program. The counselors present the certificates. Parents are encouraged to come forward and take photos or videos if they wish. Students and parents enjoy refreshments following the assembly, enjoying goodies and a chance to talk with each other. The principal arranges for an individual photo of each student and displays the photos in a designated area. Counselors submit the Student of the Month list to media.

A Student of the Month program that really makes a significant impact on students, and the school as a whole, has a number of advantages. It causes teachers to get involved in student recognition. It helps students feel that they have worth and that they do "good things." It helps parents feel that their children are special. It improves the school climate. In one school, the Student of the Month program started quietly and ended with standing room only, with a real "let's have a real party" atmosphere.

The principal provides leadership for the program by: assisting in the design of the program, communicating goals and objectives, developing the recognition procedures, and actually participating in the program. "But all this takes a lot of time." But consider the positive impact on individual students and the school.

Principals mentor the program by teaching it to faculty, students, and parents. Mentorship further teaches the program to new personnel. Mentorship explains the importance of the program to students and parents.

A simple Student of the Month program impacts minimally. A comprehensive program impacts significantly.

OTHER RECOGNITION

Take into consideration the gifts and talents of your students, and capitalize on the opportunity to recognize them both as groups and individuals. For example, a group of students creates a video for a local contest and makes it to the finals.

Celebrate. Band students can be celebrated collaboratively for a wonderful performance or individually for events like Band-o-Rama. Students participate in Soapbox Derbies or cookies sales as Scouts. Forensics to Chess Club, theatre to hatching chicks in science class, parents and community are interested in knowing what the students are up to and love reading it in the local paper.

STAFF RECOGNITION

While we often focus on our students, teachers are an important asset to the district and deserve to be recognized as well. Providing a feeling of a family atmosphere, events such as weddings, babies, and funerals bring staff together through tears of joy and sorrow. Teachers often continue their education, adding licenses and/or degrees along the way. This is often taken for granted. Celebrate.

Teachers may apply and receive a grant to earn items for their classrooms. Celebrate. A teacher may publish. Celebrate. Someone may go through specified training. Celebrate. Someone's child celebrated a major event. Celebrate. Someone became a new grandparent. Celebrate.

Through celebrating with each other, unity and relationships are built. It is important to keep lines of communication open so you remain aware of these events in people's lives. The last thing you want is for someone to be hurt because no one recognized an accomplishment when in reality it wasn't communicated.

Celebrations most often take place at staff meetings. However, depending on the event, you may very well want to bring it to the awareness of the public. This can be done at a board meeting where it becomes part of minutes or perhaps is on closed-circuit television. Many local papers have an education section or community section where school information can be shared free of charge. A short article, perhaps with a picture, can be a wonderful accolade.

STUDENT RECOGNITION—ACTIVITY

Go on an informational scavenger hunt throughout the school. What are staff members up to? How about the students? Is there anything that should be recognized? Create your list below.

Think about the programs offered by your school that celebrate student recognition. On this page, brainstorm your ideas about where you see improvements could be made and ideas for new recognition programs. Lead, mentor, and implement a new student recognition program for your school.

STUDENT ACCOMPLISHMENTS—REFLECTION

Review recognition programs in place within your school. Do these programs impact students? Positively? Are parents involved? How are accomplishments of the students shared with the community? What changes could you recommend and implement to improve the programs?

How can you create an atmosphere of celebration without creating jealousy or animosity?

What do you do with the overachiever? You know, the one who's always into something?

What do you do about the staff member who is stagnant and whose professional goal includes making it through the school year?

What do you think about recognizing staff for projects they are doing around the school?

23

Programs and Assemblies

Leading and mentoring for programs and assemblies . . . Are you kidding? Nope. Saying "Oh, yeah, that sounds cool" does not constitute leadership for school programs. Programs and assemblies require the same intense approach as other school activities, as we shall see. Take nothing for granted as you plan, communicate, and execute programs and assemblies.

A definition of program: A contracted outside individual or group performing before all, or part of, the student body. Leadership for programs first answers several questions: What is the goal of the program? Does the goal of the program match a goal of the school and the school district? Does the program reinforce established school curriculum? Does the program commemorate a special day, week, or month? Does the program motivate good school behavior? If these questions can be answered with a yes, then the program is worthy of consideration.

A school principal has resources to help identify good programs. Another principal might recommend a program. An outside school agency might ask if it can sponsor a program, such as a motivational speaker. The school district might sponsor or arrange a program that travels from school to school, such as an annual science program. A person or group might make a direct proposal, such as the PTSA securing an artist in residence. A Google of "school assemblies and programs" will lead to promotions for many diverse programs where you then ensure the goals of the agency align with the goals of the school.

The planning of programs and assemblies should be done well in advance of the date. When preparing the next year's calendar, it is wise to secure presenters for the upcoming school year. This way the dates are set, and people are informed of the programs and assemblies. One way to cause sure anxiety is "forgetting" to inform your staff of a program. Good planning and good communication of the plan help people enjoy the presentation.

The principal must arrange the method of payment for the program. If the program is a district program, it comes at district expense; otherwise it is usually up to the administration to locate funding.

There may be a line item in the budget, or creative financing may come into play. The Parent Teacher Student Association provides a good source. Some groups offer to give a free program during the school day if the school promotes and sells tickets for a paid dance/evening program. Sometimes the district may offer to pay part of the cost if the program has a reputation of being good and if there is a very close alignment of the program and district objectives. Also check other areas, such as Title I, to see if the program meets guidelines.

Method of payment must be part of the discussion when booking and confirming a program. If a contract is required, be sure to know who can sign the contract based on your district/school policies. Some performers want a deposit up front with the remainder due on the day of the performance. Be sure to plan ahead. If it takes a month for a check to be cut, figure out your time line. Some performers will allow you to be billed. Ask up front.

The principal must prepare parents, staff, and students for the program. If the program comes from outside the district, parents should know about it well in advance, just in case a parent would wish to exclude a child from attending. Staff need to know at what time of the school day the program will occur, what class period will be eliminated, what district objectives the program meets, what kind of a program it is, and the duration of the assembly. If you have a.m. and p.m. sessions, be sure to schedule so that students in each session have the opportunity to participate in some of the programs and assemblies.

Staff who know about a program are better motivated to support it. Students need to know much of what teachers know. Added is the expectation of appropriate behavior for the assembly. Answers to questions in advance set the stage for a good program.

On the day of the program, the principal must actively participate. The principal should remind students of the program during opening announcements. The principal should call students to report to the assembly place. The principal should introduce the program. The principal should supervise students during the program. And, finally, the principal should direct appropriate behavior as students return to class.

The need for the principal to be visible is important; however, the numbers and types of activities in larger schools may demand that assistant or sub-school principals, deans, or other staff members be assigned to execute some of these events, thereby calling for school leadership to work together as a team.

The principal and other staff, such as assistant principals and teachers who participated in the assembly, must evaluate the program. Questions may revolve around communication and advance preparation for the assembly. Did students respond appropriately? Was organization and planning for the program sufficient? Would you invite them back? Would you recommend them? A student survey about the program is also a good way to evaluate the program.

Assemblies, and their planning, implementation, and review, differ from programs only in their definition. Assembly means "an all school gathering designed to promote a special school event, with school staff and students as the participants."

Following the leadership behaviors for programs helps the production of a successful assembly. The principal must consider the purpose of the assembly, the content of the assembly, the planning of the assembly, and the people who have active performing roles in the assembly. Assemblies may include Homecoming, pep rallies, or beginning of the year assemblies to cover school rules and expectations.

All of the above constitute leadership.

Mentorship is teaching leadership activities for school programs to assistant principals and other administrators. All of the above could be crafted into a written district guide that all levels of administration receive annually. Simply stated, mentorship is teaching the production of a good assembly to assistant principals, staff, and students.

PROGRAMS AND ASSEMBLIES—ACTIVITY

Locate the person(s) in your district who can assist you with the following:

What is your annual budget for programs and assemblies?

Is this budget expired for the upcoming school year? If not, how much is left?

What programs and assemblies are scheduled for the current and/or upcoming school year? Who is the contact person? Have these assemblies been "marketed" appropriately?

Is there a way to get the community involved more?

Are other schools invited to attend? Could you partner up with another school?

How does the assembly or program tie in to your curriculum?

PROGRAMS AND ASSEMBLIES—REFLECTION

Think about the programs and assemblies in which you participated as a student. Which were the most memorable, and why?

Think about the programs and assemblies your students have attended over the years. Which did they talk about the most? Why were they the topic of conversation?

How would you prioritize programs and assemblies? In other words, with all of the hats you wear, how much effort do you put into aligning programs and assemblies with your curriculum and then obtaining top-notch presenters? Do you deplete your funds in this area? Who is involved in the selection: staff, PTSA, students? Take a pulse and determine if this is an area that needs improvement or not.

24

Top Ten List: "What Do You Expect from Your Supervisor?"

To develop this top ten list, we reviewed replies from thirty-one teachers who answered the question, "What do you expect from your supervisor?" Participants answered the open question using their own descriptors and shared multiple responses. There were thirty-two descriptors used, including words such as respect, honesty, and provides necessary training.

Here is your top ten list of "What do you expect from your supervisor?":

10. Feedback
9. Collaboration
8. Materials
7. Guidance
6. Approachable
5. Communication
4. Answer questions
3. Make expectations known
2. Information that affects my job

And the number one answer given:

1. Support

25

Resources and Support for the Educational Leader

Sometimes there is a misconception that we need to have all of the answers. The truth is that we don't need to know all of the answers, but we must be resourceful and be able to find the answers. We live in an age where information is at our fingertips, and it is up to us to determine credibility of the source, verification of the content, and pertinence of the information. Most districts will have an office dedicated to most areas in question; however, those that don't usually provide contact information for areas with questions.

Each state has an office dedicated to public education. It is highly recommended that you explore this resource as they often offer a wealth of information on regulations, policies, resources, and standards. The state office will often hold training sessions for new administrators to teach paperwork and remind the new administrators of deadlines and provide examples of surveys or self-reflection tools such as dpi.state.wi.us/sig/improvement/process.html.

It would be difficult to list every resource to administrators. Therefore, the list shared here is not exhaustive but merely a starting point:

Association of Supervision and Curriculum Development: ascd.org
Institute of Education Sciences (U.S. Department of Education): ies.ed.gov
National Association of Elementary School Principals: naesp.org
National Association of Secondary School Principals: www.principals.org
National Center on Response to Intervention: www.rti4success.org
National Council of Teachers of Mathematics: www.nctm.org
National High School Center: www.betterhighschools.org
National Reading Panel: www.nationalreadingpanel.org
What Works Clearinghouse (U.S. Department of Education): ies.ed.gov/ncee/wwc/publications/practiceguides

Bibliography

Achinstein, B., & Villar, A. (2004). Mentoring Relationships and New Teacher Learning: Collaboration and Complexity. *Journal of Educational Change, 5*(4), 311–344.

Bowie, L. (2010, June 9). Raise City Teacher Pay, Dismiss Poor Performers. National Group Recommends Changes to Union Contract, State Law. *Baltimore Sun.*

Brunson, J. (2008, January 14). Building Confident Leaders: Twenty-first Century Leadership Skills—Defined. Blog at WordPress.com.

Carnegie, D. (1937). Golden Book: Principles from How to Win Friends and Influence People. Dale Carnegie Training. Retrieved February 16, 2010, from www.dalecarnegie.com/flash/gbflash.htm.

Cole, B. (2005). Peak Performance in the Workplace: The New Corporate Ethic. Retrieved February 16, 2010, from www.mentalgamecoach.com.

Collins, E. (2009, March 15). Leadership Lessons from Apollo to Discovery. Speaker at ASCD Conference, San Antonio, Texas.

Conway, K. (1981, Fall). Seven Factors in Setting Career Goals. *Journal of College Placement*, 53–55.

Dalloway, M. (2009). Peak Performance Training. Retrieved February 16, 2010, from www.performance-media.com/faz.php.

Doran, G., Miller, A., & Cunningham, J. (1981). There's a S.M.A.R.T. Way to Write Management's Goals and Objectives. *Management Review, 70*(11), 35–36.

Effective Leadership Styles: Best Practices and Qualities for Today's World. (2007). Retrieved February 16, 2010, from www.what-are-good-leadership-skills.com/effective-leadership-styles.html.

Fullan, M. (2003). *Through New Eyes: Examining the Culture of Your School.* Video by Solution Tree.

Goleman, G., Boyatzis, R., & McKee, A. (2002). *Primal Leadership: Learning to Lead with Emotional Intelligence.* Boston: Harvard Business School Press.

Grzeskowiak, M. Management Styles. Retrieved February 16, 2010, from www.medhunters.com/articles/managementStyles.html.

Hales, D. (2007, February). Burned Out: Has Stress Pushed You into the Danger Zone? *Reader's Digest*, 153–57.

Juech, C. (2009, March 17). Twenty-first Century Requires New Sets of Leadership Skills. *Milwaukee Biz Blog*. Retrieved February 16, 2010, from www.biztimes.com/blogs/milwaukee-biz-blog/2009/3/17/21st-century-requires-new-kinds-of-leadership-skills.

Leadership Qualities for the Twenty-first Century. (2009). Retrieved February 16, 2010, from www.shirlawsonline.com/editorials/49-leadership-qualities-for-the-21st-century.

Lee, T. W., Locke, E. A., & Latham, G. P. (1989). Goal Setting Theory and Job Performance. In A. Pervin (Ed.), *Goal Concepts in Personality and Social Psychology* (pp. 291–326). Hillsdale, NJ: Lawrence Erlbaum.

Locke, E. A., & Latham, G. P. (1990). *A Theory of Goal Setting and Task Performance*. Englewood Cliffs, NJ: Prentice-Hall.

Locke, E. A., Shaw, K. N., Saari, L. M., & Latham, G. P. (1981). Goal Setting and Task Performance: 1969–1980. *Psychological Bulletin, 90*, 125–152.

Marcus, C. (2002). Six Characteristics for Achieving Peak Performance. Retrieved February 16, 2010, from www.cmarcus.com/pdf/Six%20Characteristics%20for%20Achieving%20Peak%20Performance.pdf.

MindTools. (2010). Locke's Goal Setting Theory: Understanding SMART Goal Setting. Retrieved February 16, 2010, from www.mindtools.com/pages/article/newHTE_87.htm.

Personality Characteristics of Peak Performers: What It Takes to be Successful. Retrieved February 15, 2010, from www.squidoo.com/selectingtalent.

Roosevelt, E. (1937). *This Is My Story*. New York: Harper.

Sandmann, L., & Vandenberg, L. (1995, December). Twenty-first Century Leadership Defined. Retrieved February 16, 2010, from www.goe.org/joe/1995december/a1.php.

Sterrett, E. (2003). I'm Supposed to Supervise These People: First Aid for Common People-Management Problems. Retrieved February 15, 2010, from www.quickwhatdoldo.com.

Ullman, E. (2009, April). Supporting Struggling Teachers. *ASCD Education Update*. Retrieved February 16, 2010, from www.ascd.org/publications/newsletters/education-update/apr09/vol51/num04/Supporting-Struggling-Teachers.aspx.

What Makes a Great Manager? (2007). Retrieved February 16, 2010, from www.GreatManager.Net.

Yearta, S, Maitlis, S., & Briner, R. (1995, September 1). An Exploratory Study of Goal Setting in Theory and Practice: A Motivational Technique that Works? *Journal of Occupational and Organizational Psychology*. Retrieved July 24, 2010, from www.highbeam.com/doc/1G1-17536457.html.

About the Authors

Kimberly T. Strike had an announcement to make at her preschool graduation ceremony. As she stepped to the microphone, she proudly announced when she grew up she wanted to be a teacher. Earning a bachelor's degree in elementary education, she fulfilled her childhood dream. She continued her education, earning a master's of education and then a doctorate from Marquette University in 2000. Her areas of study include curriculum, instruction, administration, supervision, and technology in education. Passionate about these areas, she works with teachers to increase student achievement through diagnostic-prescriptive instruction, effective mentoring, and coaching. She is renowned for her supportive nature and resourcefulness. In 2005 she was nominated as Young Alumni at Marquette University School of Education. She was also selected to serve as an Educational Ambassador to China in summer 2005. In 2006 she traveled to Russia to work with children in orphanages, and in 2009 she did the same in Uzbekistan. In 2007, she was a recipient of Phi Delta Kappa's Distinguished Leadership in Education Award.

John Nickelsen decided that he wanted to teach when he was in eighth grade. An English teacher, who obviously loved his job, helped John decide, in his junior year in high school, that he should teach English. He received his B.Ed. from the University of Wisconsin, Whitewater, in 1964. What followed was a career as ninth-grade English teacher, which lasted nineteen years. He taught all during that time at Mitchell Junior High School of the Racine, Wisconsin, Unified School District. In addition to teaching English skills to his students, he encouraged them to express themselves well in writing on their own, to draw their own conclusions about what they read, and to think for themselves. He also designed and taught a unit featuring Wisconsin writers. John received his M.S. in educational administration and supervision from the University of Wisconsin, Milwaukee, in 1969. He served as an assistant principal at McKinley Middle School in Racine for seven years. During that time, he worked at integrating the sixth-grade students into the school, as the district had changed from junior high schools to middle schools. He helped integrate the students of the gifted-talented program into the mainstream of the student body. He also specialized as the school scheduler. As sub-school principal of Washington Park High School in Racine, he specialized in school security. As principal of Mitchell Middle School, also in Racine, he emphasized the importance of a strong student-services department. As a retired educator, he has served the Racine Unified School District as a substitute administrator and a test proctor. In the late seventies, John wrote and published "Romeo and Juliet, a Study Text."

www.ingramcontent.com/pod-product-compliance
Lightning Source LLC
Chambersburg PA
CBHW080939300426
44115CB00017B/2877